What Your Colleagues Are Saying . .

As needs, demands, interests, and opportunities for online instruction increase, *Culturally Responsive Teaching Online and In Person* is a book that will assist educators in the complex task of designing essential learning opportunities with students for academic and social success. This book reminds us that culturally responsive teaching practices are potentially transformative in person and online. Indeed, this book helps educators think about the tools, technology, and teaching necessary to build more liberating, humanizing, and just spaces of education.

---**H. Richard Milner IV**
Distinguished Professor, Vanderbilt University
Co-Author, *These Kids Are Out of Control*

For more than 30 years, scholars and educators have advocated for the importance of centering students' cultural frames into the co-learning exchange of all learners, but in particular, Black and Brown students, who have been historically marginalized in educational settings. The distinction of Budhai and Grant's critically important book: *Culturally Responsive Teaching Online & In Person*, is the argument that culturally responsive teaching (CRT) is not just for in-person instruction, but moreover, CRT can also be facilitated within an online modality. Thus, this book is a seminal resource for PK–12 educators who are passionate about reimagining the possibilities of CRT in any learning environment!

--**Ronald W. Whitaker II**
Culturally Responsive Assistant Professor of Education
Director of the Center for Urban Education, Equity, and Improvement, Cabrini University

Budhai and Grant have created a treasure trove of resources for K–12 teachers and teacher educators who are committed to transforming a rapidly changing world for the better. Finally, we have a book that concretizes how to maximize culturally relevant pedagogy in contemporary, HyFlex learning environments in real time. This text helps the reader translate the philosophical into the practical via inquiry-based, reflective exercises. This book will empower educators, leading them to create equitably rich opportunities for deep and dynamic learning across modalities. The cornerstone of this text, the Dynamic Equitable Learning Environments (DELE) model, inspires a new way of teaching and learning in the 21st century, providing new pathways to transform our schools by challenging and changing ourselves. As we shift our mindset to realize that we can change systems by recognizing the barriers to equity and inclusion, we reimagine an education that realizes justice in our classrooms, anti-racism in society, and healing in our homes. You will read and reread the gems of culturally responsive teaching and build your capacity to sustain equitable and thriving learning environments for our students to thrive in a world where their lives truly matter.

—**Angela N. Campbell**
Vice President of Cabrini University

I joyfully offer my endorsement of *Culturally Responsive Teaching Online & In Person*. At this critical moment in human history, scholars need a resource like this to be equipped with the tools that will empower teaching and learning at its fullness. Budhai and Grant prove their scholarship in this work, especially by posing questions that lead to critical thinking. As an educator and a life-long learner, I plan to use this work and invite others to join me.

—**Stephen D. Thorne**
Center for Research and Mentoring of Black Male Students and Teachers
Bowie State University

As teaching and learning environments continue to evolve at a breakneck pace, this wonderfully accessible guide is chock full of practical, useful, and actionable advice to help educators successfully navigate their culturally diverse classrooms, schools, and education communities. With self-guided exercises and reflections, educators are able to address their unconscious biases, make meaningful connections with families and students, and ultimately, effectively incorporate culturally responsive teaching as they build the dynamic and equitable learning environments necessary for all students to thrive. Required reading for every educator!

—**Ray Benedici**
Managing Editor, *Tech & Learning*

This workbook is a much-needed resource that attracts, engages, and supports teacher candidates, as cultural beings, in their transformation to becoming culturally aware, responsive, and humble educators. The authors position future educators to identify, acknowledge, and reflect on the critical role of their evolving racial and cultural identities and the implications thereof when practicing in the classroom. The book is a resource that transcends theory into practice and will serve teacher candidates in their journey as equity-minded practitioners to effectively implement culturally responsive, relevant, and sustaining pedagogies.

—**Omobolade Delano-Oriara**
Dean of the Division of Social Sciences, Professor of Teacher Education
St. Norbert College

Our students and their communities need educators who are courageous enough to acknowledge the role race plays as a barrier to learning. Our work is not universally designed if we lack the willingness to address race and racism and the need for culturally responsive teaching, regardless of whether or not we are engaging students virtually or in person. Budhai and Grant, through this text, are pushing us to do better for our young scholars by calling out the fact that our systems, structures, and practices need to be culturally relevant if they are to authentically include and center around our learners who have been historically marginalized. This is a wonderful resource that guides educators step by step through the process of developing and implementing culturally responsive practices, virtually and in person.

—**Mirko Chardin**
Chief Equity and Inclusion Officer, Novak Education
Co-Author, *Equity by Design*

This guidebook addresses many questions and needs for educators to operationalize culturally responsive teaching across learning environments, in person and online. I appreciate that the guidebook unpacks the work of Ladson-Billings, Gay, and Paris by connecting the theory to practice. I recommend this book for educators who actively engage in anti-bias, equitable, inclusive, and just teaching. The reflection questions, checklists, resources, and exercises are tangible actions for educators to engage in moving toward actions in their environments.

—**Robert Q. Berry III**
Samuel Braley Gray Professor of Mathematics Education
Associate Dean of Diversity, Equity, & Inclusion
University of Virginia, School of Education & Human Development

Culturally Responsive Teaching
Online & In Person

From Stephanie:

To every student whose voice has been silenced in school.

To every student who could not see themselves in the curriculum.

To every student who has never felt like they matter to their teachers.

★ ★ ★ ★

From Kristine:

For my students past, present, and future–
It is my honor to teach and learn with and from each of you.

Culturally Responsive Teaching
Online & In Person

An Action Planner for
Dynamic
Equitable
Learning
Environments

Stephanie Smith Budhai

Kristine S. Lewis Grant

Foreword by Matthew R. Kay

FOR INFORMATION:

Corwin

A SAGE Company

2455 Teller Road

Thousand Oaks, California 91320

(800) 233-9936

www.corwin.com

SAGE Publications Ltd.

1 Oliver's Yard

55 City Road

London EC1Y 1SP

United Kingdom

SAGE Publications India Pvt. Ltd.

B 1/I 1 Mohan Cooperative Industrial Area

Mathura Road, New Delhi 110 044

India

SAGE Publications Asia-Pacific Pte. Ltd.

18 Cross Street #10-10/11/12

China Square Central

Singapore 048423

President: Mike Soules

Associate Vice President and Editorial Director: Monica Eckman

Executive Editor: Tori Mello Bachman

Content Development Editor: Sharon Wu

Editorial Assistant: Nancy Chung

Project Editor: Amy Schroller

Copy Editor: Deanna Noga

Typesetter: C&M Digitals (P) Ltd.

Proofreader: Dennis Webb

Cover Designer: Janet Kiesel

Marketing Manager: Margaret O'Connor

Copyright © 2022 by Stephanie Smith Budhai and Kristine S. Lewis Grant

All rights reserved. Except as permitted by U.S. copyright law, no part of this work may be reproduced or distributed in any form or by any means, or stored in a database or retrieval system, without permission in writing from the publisher.

When forms and sample documents appearing in this work are intended for reproduction, they will be marked as such. Reproduction of their use is authorized for educational use by educators, local school sites, and/or noncommercial or nonprofit entities that have purchased the book.

All third-party trademarks referenced or depicted herein are included solely for the purpose of illustration and are the property of their respective owners. Reference to these trademarks in no way indicates any relationship with, or endorsement by, the trademark owner.

Printed in the United States of America

Library of Congress Cataloging-in-Publication Data

Names: Budhai, Stephanie Smith, author. | Grant, Kristine S. Lewis, author.

Title: Culturally responsive teaching online and in person : an action planner for dynamic equitable learning environments / Stephanie Smith Budhai, Kristine S. Lewis Grant ; foreword by Matthew R. Kay.

Description: Thousand Oaks, California : Corwin, 2022. | Series: Corwin teaching essentials | Includes bibliographical references and index.

Identifiers: LCCN 2021049212 | ISBN 9781071855270 (paperback) | ISBN 9781071873335 (epub) | ISBN 9781071873342 (epub) | ISBN 9781071873359 (pdf)

Subjects: LCSH: Culturally relevant pedagogy—United States. | Web-based instruction—Social aspects—United States.

Classification: LCC LC1099.3 .B83 2022 | DDC 370.1170973—dc23/eng/20211116

LC record available at https://lccn.loc.gov/2021049212

This book is printed on acid-free paper.

22 23 24 25 26 10 9 8 7 6 5 4 3 2 1

DISCLAIMER: This book may direct you to access third-party content via Web links, QR codes, or other scannable technologies, which are provided for your reference by the author(s). Corwin makes no guarantee that such third-party content will be available for your use and encourages you to review the terms and conditions of such third-party content. Corwin takes no responsibility and assumes no liability for your use of any third-party content, nor does Corwin approve, sponsor, endorse, verify, or certify such third-party content.

Contents

PART III: FOCUSING ON YOUR PEDAGOGICAL PRACTICES: INCORPORATING CULTURALLY RELEVANT TEACHING   113

Foreword

As recent years have brought an increased awareness of inequities in our world, our nation, and our schools, it's become increasingly popular for many of us to loudly proclaim that we are *doing the work*. While we've always been a culture that celebrates grit and grind, the high-profile nature of recent injustices has made activism much more palatable and resistance more Instagrammable. These trends hold true in education. In many schools, teachers have found attempts to be culturally responsive celebrated for the first time in a long time. In others, efforts that were once ignored face vilification. Either way, *the work* has certainly become an attention grabber.

This attention has come with reduced clarity. The more we opine about the work, the fewer people of good will agree on what it is. For instance, should educators have used the disruptions caused by the Covid pandemic to thoroughly dismantle systems that have been poisoned by racist, sexist, xenophobic, and/or homophobic ideas? Or should we have devised better ways to destabilize such systems from within? To what degree should the Western (read "White, male") literary canon be deemphasized to make room for more diverse voices? How do we best teach truth in our social studies classes, acknowledging that generations have long substituted idolization for historical analysis? *The work* is confusing, even before we educators make it more personal. What right do *we* have to lead *that* conversation? Are we even *qualified*? Should our students trust us? Do our administrators have our backs as we make mistakes? Considering how damaging these mistakes might be to students' psyche, should they? For educators, the work is no less hard, no less complex, no less frightening simply because it is en vogue.

Stephanie Smith Budhai and Kristine S. Lewis Grant have written a guidebook that not only acknowledges this reality, but then strips away the noise and helps educators get down to business. From the first pages, their prompts for reflection are incisive, their exercises are both challenging and encouraging, and they lead us to create action plans meant to drive us toward concrete goals. Within minutes of picking it up, I was inspired to examine how some of my unconscious biases might have impacted certain students' performance during the 2020–2021's season of virtual schooling. These examinations helped me approach these students more productively than I would otherwise have approached them. This process repeated itself throughout my time with this text; first I reflected alone, then I did exercises collaboratively with trusted colleagues, and then finally I executed plans that improved my relationships with a variety of my students. I am a better teacher because this book makes *the work* not *easy* but clear as crystal.

Many activities in this text illustrate Budhai's and Grant's commitment to clarity. For instance, early in the book, we are encouraged to collect data on our own everyday teaching practices. This is a hard exercise that takes our heads out of the cloud-realm of high theory and simply asks, "Who do we call on?" "Who do we discipline? For what infractions? Leading to what penalty?" We are asked to find patterns, reflect on them, and address anything untoward that we discover. The most lasting systemic improvements start not with top-down initiatives, but with the uncelebrated *work* of teachers collecting data like this in their own classrooms. Only with this information, rooted in day-in and day-out student experiences, can we see clearly where we should be committing our energies.

But one of the best things about this guidebook is that it does not just ask us to tackle the ugly parts of our nature that, if unchecked, stand to poison our teaching practice. The exercises do not treat us as irredeemable racists but as caring professionals who are honing our craft. This is clearest in Part II, where we are coached on how to make sure that both our students and their families know just how much we value their particular strengths and traditions as well as they know ours; and in Part III, where we are coached in practical approaches to equity-minded, anti-bias instruction. So often, folks teaching you *why* to do the *work* never really get to the *how* part. Budhai and Grant make the *how* their home base throughout, with every reflection, exercise, and action plan in the guidebook. Their respect for educators is clear, frankly, because they don't lean on the crutch of patronizing lectures when the task seems too heavy. This book just guides us through, step by step.

I am simultaneously happy that this guidebook exists *and* happy that you have decided to use it as you start (or continue) *the work* of making your classroom all that your students deserve it to be. It is not easy, but it is necessary. It will not always be attention-grabbing in the larger world, but it will always be what your students pay most attention to, and what they most remember. Take your time with this book, being honest with yourself, your colleagues, and especially your students. Trust me, your humility and effort will pay off.

—Matthew R. Kay
Teacher and author of *Not Light, But Fire*

Acknowledgments

FROM STEPHANIE

Thank you to the Budhai, Smith, and Macon families for the continued support and love. There is no way this book would have been able to come to fruition without you.

I would like to thank my co-author, Kristine, for the mentorship, advisement, and perspective that she has brought to this project. I cannot think of a better person to have engaged in this work with, and I am grateful for her time and talents.

To Sharon, I am beyond beholden to the amount of care and consideration you have given to this project. Your timely responses and substantive suggestions have elevated this project to a level unimaginable.

And to Tori, thank you for not abandoning us and for your continued commitment to see this project to completion. You are one of a kind, and I feel lucky to have had the opportunity to work with you.

To the educators who have shared their stories featured in the vignettes; THANK YOU! Your experiences have provided so rich context for readers as they navigate the contents of this book.

I would be remiss if I did not acknowledge the thought leaders, activists, and educators who have created a pathway for culturally responsive pedagogy to be an integral part of teaching and learning. Many of whom have been cited in this book, and there are too many others whose work lives in other publications and is carried out in classrooms having a direct impact on the schooling experience of students.

FROM KRISTINE

Stephanie, this would not have been possible without you. From the bottom of my heart, thank you.

Jermaine, thank you for supporting and believing in me. I could not have done this without you.

PUBLISHER'S ACKNOWLEDGMENT

Corwin gratefully acknowledges the contributions of the following reviewer:

Crystal Wash
School Principal, CERA
Chicago, IL

A Note From the Publisher on Terminology

The grammar conventions in this book follow The Chicago Manual of Style. *The authors and publisher did our best to represent current terminology at the time of printing, while recognizing that the English language is ever changing and will continue to evolve after this book's publication. For example, certain terms appear with and without hyphenation across sources, such as "in person" vs. "in-person" and "equity mindedness" vs. "equity-mindedness." Following* The Chicago Manual of Style, *we've chosen to omit the hyphenation when the term is a noun ("in person" and "equity mindedness") and include the hyphenation when the term is transformed into and used as an adjective ("in-person" and "equity-minded instruction").*

About the Authors

Stephanie Smith Budhai, PhD is an associate clinical professor at Drexel University and a certified K–12 teacher. She has spent the past decade as a teacher educator building culturally responsive and anti-racist curriculum. She is on the board of the Pennsylvania Chapter of the National Association for Multicultural Education.

Kristine S. Lewis Grant, PhD is a clinical professor of multicultural and urban education at Drexel University. Her research interests include family engagement in urban schools and the recruitment and retention of teachers of color. She is a board member of the Pennsylvania chapter of the National Association for Multicultural Education.

Introduction
Why Culturally Responsive Teaching Matters in Dynamic Equitable Learning Environments

WHY THIS BOOK? WHY YOU?

Welcome to *Culturally Responsive Teaching Online and In Person*!

The purpose of this guidebook is to serve as an interactive workspace and instructional tool for teacher preparation and professional development. The goals of the book include (a) building teachers' self-awareness and cultural competence through critical reflection, (b) enhancing teachers' knowledge and skills related to culturally responsive pedagogy, and (c) applying online instructional tools and strategies to create culturally responsive environments across in-person and online learning settings. This book will enable PK–12 educators to meaningfully engage with all their students in any classroom setting and ensure that the entire class is an engaging and equitable environment for all. This is the first book of its kind to address culturally responsive teaching across both in-person and online learning settings.

Stop and Reflect: What's Your Why?

Before we dive further into the context of this guidebook, please take a moment to contemplate why you are beginning this guidebook. In the space below, explain three reasons why you are interested in learning more about culturally responsive teaching in both in-person and online learning environments.

(Continued)

(Continued)

1.
2.
3.

Chances are that one of your primary reasons for reading this book is for your students.

FOR OUR STUDENTS

In the United States, PK–12 students are becoming more racially and ethnically diverse (de Brey et al., 2019). For the past decade, the National Center for Educational Statistics has documented the shift in student demographics. Between fall 2009 and fall 2018, the percentages of White and Black students decreased (7 percentage points and 2 percentage points, respectively), while the percentages of Latinx* students and students of two or more races increased (5 percentage points and 3 percentage points, respectively). The percentages of Asian, Pacific Islander, Indigenous students remained largely unchanged during this same time period. In fall 2018, of the 50.7 million students enrolled in public elementary and secondary schools, White students accounted for 47 percent of the student population, Black students accounted for 15 percent, Latinx students accounted

---

*Authors' Note on Terminology

We understand that culturally responsive language is constantly changing and evolving. In our book, we chose to use the term *Latinx* as a broad gender-neutral term for peoples of Latin American descent. We acknowledge that some people do not embrace this term, and we understand that the context and conversation around this term continue to change.

for 27 percent, Asian students accounted for 5 percent, and Indigenous students accounted for 1 percent. Students who were of two or more races accounted for 4 percent, and Pacific Islander students accounted for less than one half of 1 percent. Taken together, students of color comprised 53 percent of the U.S. public school classrooms. To see tables depicting these and other relevant student demographics, please visit the National Center for Education Statistics website.

Scan this QR code to view figures of student demographics from the National Center for Education Statistics.

Despite this shift in student demographics and new promises of change, educational inequities and disparities stubbornly remain. And quite frankly, and eloquently put by Kay (2018), "with little regard for substance of coherence, we find our airwaves filled with empty rhetoric and thoughtless repetition" (p. 12). Students of color are more likely to attend high-poverty, racially segregated schools than their White peers (de Brey et al., 2019). Per pupil spending is significantly less in high poverty, racially segregated schools than it is in low poverty, predominantly White schools (Baker & Corcoran, 2012; Mathewson, 2020). Related to these structural inequities, academic disparities endure. Students of color do not perform as well on standardized tests in math and reading as their White counterparts (Carnoy & Garcia, 2017). While gaps in the high school graduation rate have been slowly closing since 2000, students of color are still less likely to graduate than their White peers (The Condition of Education, 2021).

Given these and related racial inequities and educational disparities, culturally responsive teaching has gained momentum within schools across the country as a viable pedagogy to improve equitable access, opportunities, and learning outcomes for culturally and linguistically diverse students. School districts and state departments of education from California to New York have adopted, wholeheartedly or in part, culturally responsive teaching practices for their faculty and staff.

Stop and Reflect: Obstacles and Possibilities of Culturally Responsive Teaching

In your own words, what are 2–3 obstacles to your adoption of culturally responsive practices in in-person and online learning environments? What are 2–3 possibilities for your adoption of culturally responsive teaching in in-person and online learning environments?

(Continued)

(Continued)

	OBSTACLES	POSSIBILITIES
Culturally responsive teaching in IN-PERSON learning environments	1.	1.
	2.	2.
	3.	3.
Culturally responsive teaching in ONLINE learning environments	1.	1.
	2.	2.
	3.	3.

Unfortunately, culturally responsive teaching is largely understood as a strategy for traditional in-person classrooms, and irrelevant for online learning environments. This book aims to help you overcome perceived obstacles to culturally responsive teaching regardless of the learning environment, and pursue the possibilities of culturally responsive teaching in any educational setting.

As a PK–12 teacher in today's sociopolitical context, do you feel prepared to engage your culturally and linguistically diverse students and their families across a range of learning environments? Are you prepared to integrate cultural content and themes of equity and social justice into your curriculum and instruction regardless of the learning context? Are you prepared to employ a culturally responsive and equity-minded approach to your relationships with your students in different classroom settings? If you are uncertain in your responses to these questions, this is the book for you.

WHAT IS CULTURALLY RESPONSIVE TEACHING?

Ladson-Billings (1994) defined culturally relevant pedagogy as one "that empowers students intellectually, socially, emotionally, and politically using cultural referents to impart knowledge, skills, and attitudes" (pp. 16–17). Her framework (1994) is based on her research of effective teachers of African American students. Ladson-Billings (2014) identified three domains that were present in all their teaching practices:

- **Academic success:** the intellectual growth that students experience as a result of classroom instruction and learning experiences.

- **Cultural competence:** the ability to help students appreciate and celebrate their cultures of origin while gaining knowledge of and fluency in at least one other culture.

- **Sociopolitical consciousness:** the ability to take learning beyond the confines of the classroom using school knowledge and skills to identify, analyze, and solve real-world problems. (p. 75)

By adopting these domains in their practice, culturally relevant pedagogues can help "students to recognize and honor their own cultural beliefs and practices while acquiring access to the wider culture, where they are likely to have a chance of improving their socioeconomic status and making informed decisions about the lives they wish to lead" (Ladson-Billings, 2006, p. 36).

Gay (2010) defined culturally responsive teaching "as using the cultural knowledge, prior experiences, frames of reference, and performance styles of ethnically diverse students to make learning encounters more relevant to and effective for them" (p. 31). Culturally responsive teaching is based on six dimensions:

1. Culturally responsive teachers are socially and academically empowering by setting high expectations for students with a commitment to every student's success;

2. Culturally responsive teachers are multidimensional because they engage cultural knowledge, experiences, contributions, and perspectives;

3. Culturally responsive teachers validate every student's culture, bridging gaps between school and home through diversified instructional strategies and multicultural curricula;

4. Culturally responsive teachers are socially, emotionally, and politically comprehensive as they seek to educate the whole child;

5. Culturally responsive teachers are transformative of schools and societies by using students' existing strengths to drive instruction, assessment, and curriculum design;

6. Culturally responsive teachers are emancipatory and liberating from oppressive educational practices and ideologies as they lift "the veil of presumed absolute authority from conceptions of scholarly truth typically taught in schools." (Gay, 2010, p. 38)

Culturally responsive teaching requires educators to develop the following areas in service of student learning: self-awareness, instructional techniques, instructional materials, student-teacher relationships, and classroom climate.

Paris (2012) expanded on the work of culturally relevant pedagogy to develop culturally sustaining pedagogy. Paris and Alim (2014) presented a "loving critique" of culturally relevant pedagogy and other asset-based pedagogies, along three lines:

1. The need for asset pedagogies to sustain the cultural and linguistic practices of communities of color for a pluralist present and future

2. The need for asset pedagogies to sustain the cultural and linguistic practices of communities of color in ways that reflect our increasingly fluid understanding of the evolving relations between language, culture, race, and ethnicity

3. Creating generative spaces for asset pedagogies to support the practices of youth and communities of color while maintaining a critical lens vis-a-vis these practices. (p. 92)

The goals of culturally sustaining pedagogy include "supporting multilingualism and multiculturalism in practice and perspective for students and teachers" and "to perpetuate and foster—to sustain—linguistic, literate, and cultural pluralism as part of the democratic project of schooling and as a needed response to demographic and social change" (Paris & Alim, 2014, p. 88). The tenets of this framework read:

> a focus on the plural and evolving nature of youth identity and cultural practices and a commitment to embracing youth culture's counterhegemonic potential while maintaining a clear-eyed critique of the ways in which youth culture can also reproduce systemic inequalities. (Paris & Alim, 2014, p. 85)

Stop and Reflect: Hallmark Characteristics of a Classroom

What are the hallmark characteristics of a PK–12 classroom? Close your eyes for a few moments and imagine a classroom. Use the space below to either draw a diagram of the classroom or to write a description.

WHAT ARE DYNAMIC EQUITABLE LEARNING ENVIRONMENTS?

In the space above, you likely imagined desks in parallel rows or arranged in small clusters. If not desks, perhaps you envisioned tables with chairs assembled in small work groups of four students. Does your image feature lab stations, reading nooks, and/or bookcases? Did you include chalkboards, Whiteboards, and/or bulletin boards? Were the walls also adorned with calendars, posters (key historical figures, maps, timelines, inspirational quotes, etc.), and/or examples of student work? Together, these are all hallmarks of a PK–12 classroom in the United States and many places around the world.

These and other elements most certainly comprise a classroom, but this is just one type of learning environment in the twenty-first century. For example, many classrooms are virtual. According to the National Education Policy Center, in 2019–2020, 332,379 students were enrolled in 477 full-time virtual schools and 152,530 students were enrolled in 306 blended schools (Molnar et al., 2021). Depending on the learning management system, features of virtual classrooms include announcement pages, weekly modules, live and recorded video presentations, video conferencing, digital Whiteboards, breakout rooms, screen sharing, chat boxes, and polls. Together, these and other elements comprise the hallmark characteristics of a virtual classroom.

Today, teaching and learning are far more flexible than in years past, and the classroom has adapted to accommodate this fluidity. Teaching and learning exist as a continuum, with in-person to online on either end and a mix of the two options in between (hybrid, simultaneous, flex, etc.). The technological tools of online learning are not limited to the virtual classroom and can be used to transform in-person learning in many creative and innovative ways. Education is no longer confined to the traditional school day within the four walls of a classroom in a brick-and-mortar building. Now, teaching and learning can take place anytime and anywhere with a stable internet connection via mobile phone, tablet, laptop, or desktop computer. To convey this change in the twenty-first century classroom, we refer to this space as a *Dynamic Equitable Learning Environment* (DELE). Figure A depicts the characteristics of DELEs.

Figure A • Characteristics of DELEs

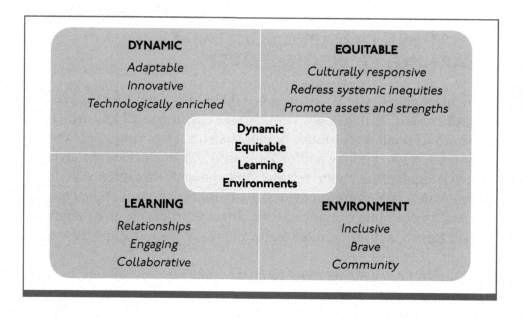

DELE is a central, original concept of this book that encompasses the design and delivery of culturally responsive pedagogy and practices within in-person and online learning environments. DELE describes a dynamic approach to the nimbleness that teachers need to possess to be culturally responsive to all learners, regardless of learning context. DELE provides a mechanism for teachers to pivot instruction and carry out the constructs of culturally responsive teaching when students are in the physical classroom space with them or in virtual learning environments. DELE enables teachers to foster equitable learning environments that promote students' assets and strengths and redress systemic inequities. DELE requires that teachers establish and sustain caring relationships with students and their families to engage students in active and collaborative learning. DELE is inclusive of all students. These spaces cultivate a learning community where students feel safe to be themselves, take academic risks, and engage in brave conversations about issues of race and social justice. Teachers who can successfully navigate through DELE can quickly pivot instruction to facilitate equitable and inclusive learning experiences for all PK–12 students.

ORGANIZATION OF THE BOOK

Key Features

The academic and social-emotional needs of culturally and linguistically diverse students were present when they attended brick-and-mortar schools, and these needs have been amplified with the nationwide move to online teaching and learning. Culturally responsive pedagogy can help educators address the academic and social-emotional needs of culturally and linguistically diverse students. By getting to know students and their families, establishing affirming learning communities, and incorporating cultural content into the curriculum, PK–12 educators can co-construct engaging in-person and online learning environments for all students. This book features checklists and repositories of culturally responsive resources to complement its contents. There are seven recurring items present in each part and/or chapter of the book as follows.

- **Virtual Equitable and Inclusive Vignettes.** These include current and authentic vignettes from PK–12 teachers who have successfully implemented aspects of culturally responsive teaching into their in-person and online classrooms that are grounded in equity and inclusion.

- **Reflection Questions.** Each chapter starts with overarching reflection questions related to the chapter's content. There is space for you to jot down your responses. At the end of the chapter, similar reflection questions are posed. You are asked to jot down your responses and then revisit your earlier responses prior to reading the chapter and note changes.

- **Examples of DELE.** Each chapter includes an example of how teachers can pivot across DELE to provide culturally responsive learning experiences for all students.

- **Anti-Bias Exercises.** Each chapter features an anti-bias exercise related to the content of the chapter that you can engage in to help further develop and understand the presented concepts.

- **Action Plans.** Each chapter includes partially pre-filled action plans that you will complete after going through the chapter's contents. The action plans serve as the next step in your path to implementing some aspect of culturally responsive pedagogy into any learning setting. You can find each chapter's action plan on the companion website.

- **Culturally Sustaining Checklists.** After reading the chapter, this section provides you with a list of action items that you should be starting to incorporate into your culturally responsive classrooms, organized by the awareness, knowledge, and skills you have gained from the respective chapter. You can find each chapter's Culturally Sustaining Checklist on the companion website.

- **Responsive Resources.** Each chapter includes a combination of the following resources (websites, podcasts, articles, and videos, etc.) that can assist you with being culturally responsive educators. You can find each chapter's Responsive Resources on the companion website.

Structure

This guidebook is divided into three parts, with three chapters in each.

Part I, "Focusing on You: Unmasking Bias and Microaggressions," requires you to engage in critical self-examination. Chapter 1, "Acknowledging Unconscious Bias," focuses on acknowledging the unconscious bias that we may bring to the teaching and learning environments. This chapter provides a foundational understanding of how our ideas, beliefs, and perspectives impact the way in which we educate learners, even without us knowing. Chapter 2, "Reducing Implicit Bias and Explicit Bias," guides you through the examination of your own biases. The goal of Chapter 2 is to help you provide equitable access and opportunities to minoritized and marginalized students through the reduction of the impact of your implicit and explicit biases. Chapter 3, "Eliminating Microaggressions," defines microaggression and describes the different forms that microaggressions can take in both online and in-person learning environments. You are provided with approaches and strategies to use microresistance and microinterventions to eliminate microaggressions.

Part II, "Focusing on Your Relationships: Co-Constructing Meaningful Connections With Students and Families," focuses on the relationships central to the work of education. Chapter 4, "Activating Students' Assets and Cultural Capital," provides the content and practice you need to value and honor the assets of all your students in DELEs. You will explore the Community Cultural Wealth model, asset-mapping, and other strengths-based approaches to teaching. Chapter 5, "Caring for Students Within Their Sociopolitical Contexts," introduces you to intersectionality and how students' multiple identities shape their educational experiences. The chapter also helps you appreciate students' experiences more fully by understanding their sociopolitical context and how this context shapes their experiences inside and outside of school. In Chapter 6, "Forging Reciprocal Relationships With Families and Communities," you examine your relationships with culturally and linguistically diverse families and communities. By drawing on the principles of culturally responsive pedagogy, you develop the necessary insight and skills to establish and sustain meaningful relationships with the core people in your students' lives.

Part III, "Focusing on Your Pedagogical Practices: Incorporating Culturally Relevant Teaching," addresses thinking about and designing culturally responsive and equitable curriculum, instruction, and assessment. Chapter 7, "Developing Equity Mindedness," discusses the ways in which you can shift their mindsets toward equity and justice. This chapter describes the ways you can build an anti-racist online and in-person class culture and environment. Chapter 8, "Planning Anti-Bias Instruction," explains how you can curate culturally relevant curriculum materials and teach students in ways that speak to their learning styles and backgrounds, and from varied perspectives. Chapter 9, "Preparing Culturally Responsive Authentic Assessments," focuses on creating authentic assessments for all our students. The chapter recommends ways to assess the learning that has taken place within our culturally relevant online and in-person classrooms.

Taken together, these three parts introduce you to reflective and practical approaches to culturally responsive instruction across any educational setting. Within these pages, you will find support with the adoption and implementation of culturally responsive approaches, strategies, and practices into your own teaching. This book provides you with a toolkit that will not only inspire you but also help translate your care and concern for students into your in-person and online classrooms.

Stop and Reflect: Three Hopes

Before we dive further into the context of this guidebook, please take a moment to articulate your intentions. In the space below, please list three things (knowledge, skills, attitudes) that you hope to develop as a result of completing this guidebook.

1.

2.

3.

Now that you have set your intentions and listed three things that you hope to learn, let's get to work!

PART ONE

Focusing on You
Unmasking Bias and Microaggressions

Vignette: Mr. Malcolm Williams

Media Teacher, Grades K–8

2020 was my second year teaching, but my first year as a full-time teacher. Like many teachers, I started teaching online for the first time because of the pandemic. If I could choose, I would prefer to teach in person, but I know that we'll continue using online settings in some capacity, even beyond the pandemic. We all have to adapt, especially as teachers.

Like any teacher, I inadvertently bring unconscious bias into both virtual and in-person classrooms, but I have a number of methods for addressing these biases. First, I try to acknowledge unconscious bias by replaying in my head what I said to my students. Reflection allows me to check myself, to think in the moment, and to think afterward. Second, I try to step into other peoples' shoes when I am talking to them. Sometimes I think what I am saying is fine but to the other person, my words can be offensive. If I can try to understand the other person's perspective, I can hear my own biases and work on them. Third, I try to read other people's reactions, both students and other adults. Asking a person directly about their feelings does not always garner a genuine response, but by reading the room for unspoken clues, I can better gauge if I may be causing offense or treating people unfairly.

I have seen many microaggressions take place between teachers and students. Some teachers are sharp with students in a way that is hurtful on a visceral level. I see teachers give feedback like "You should have done it on time," in a way that is degrading. Students do not know how to respond, and it makes them feel stupid. These moments are dangerous because students internalize these messages in a subconscious way, but do not have the correct tools to process them.

I also often see microaggressions take place between colleagues. These are damaging in a different way because adults are perhaps better equipped to handle these moments but that does not make them any less painful. Even still, adults also often internalize the aggression with no outlet to direct that pain.

In online settings, I try to check in with my students before instruction starts. It gives everyone an opportunity to get their feelings out so that they don't fester. It also brings students closer together when they're given the space to open up.

In in-person settings, I think it's easier to build community. I think it is important to take time to get to know the students in your environment and to make them feel comfortable. Students do their best work when they feel comfortable, and I think the best way to create comfortable environments is to make sure students know that they are heard, understood, and cared for. You can reduce the occurrence of unconscious bias and microaggression when you get to know your students on an individual, personal level. But it's important to be proactive and to continue working at building space for your students to grow relationships, with each other and with their teachers.

CHAPTER ONE

Acknowledging Unconscious Bias

REFLECTION QUESTIONS

Before delving into Chapter I's contents, take a few minutes to work through the following reflection questions. There is space provided below for your responses. We revisit variations of these reflection questions at the end of the chapter.

- How do I define unconscious bias?

- What stereotypes do I have about students based on their race/ethnicity, gender, or family income level?

- How can my own bias impact teaching and learning?

- What do I hope to learn from this chapter?

_____

_____

_____

_____

_____

_____

_____

WHY A FOCUS ON *UNCONSCIOUS* BIAS?

This chapter focuses on acknowledging the unconscious bias that we may bring to the teaching and learning environment. This is the first chapter of this book and provides a foundational understanding of how our ideas, beliefs, and perspectives impact the way in which we educate learners, even without us knowing. As you get into the subsequent chapters of the book, you will likely reflect on the acknowledgment of bias that you uncovered about yourself in this chapter and use this new awareness and knowledge in your future work with students across Dynamic Equitable Learning Environments (DELE).

You may be thinking to yourself, "But I am an educator! I came to this work with a full heart and treat all my students equally." The reality is, educators are people too and are not shielded from developing bias. According to Starck et al. (2020), "the current research shows that teachers' racial attitudes largely reflect those held within their broader society" (p. 281). This means that, even though we as teachers believe and want to treat all students equitably, we all bring bias that is learned from a very young age because they are situated within our minds, and unfortunately, they unintentionally impact our behaviors (Fiarman & Benson, 2020). Our bias can permeate into different situations that have long-term effects on our students. For example, research has shown that bias can impact how letters of recommendation for students are crafted, based on biases that the author of the letter has regarding different genders and ethnic backgrounds (Akos & Kretchmar, 2016). Recommendation letters are gateways to special magnet programs, special admissions high schools, elite summer STEM programs, and colleges. Thus, when our bias is impacting the content within the letters, the impact on students can be life changing.

In this chapter, we provide you with the content and practice needed to acknowledge unconscious biases that you may have in an effort to create DELE by:

- Defining unconscious bias and identifying different types of bias that can shape in-person and online learning environments

- Exploring common stereotypes that educators may bring to the classroom and providing ideas on how to stifle them

- Demonstrating how bias can show up in education contexts and discussing this impact on teaching and learning

- Reflecting on one's own unconscious bias and practicing teacher self-awareness strategies

We ask that you have a willingness to sit with discomfort as you go through the chapter. We encourage you to take advantage of the different opportunities to reflect and engage through the various anti-bias exercises. The ultimate goal is to leave this chapter with a greater awareness of how your past thinking can impact your teaching and to use culturally responsive teaching practices as a mechanism to fight against bias.

TYPES OF BIAS

The word *bias* may be a term that you are familiar with. Having a bias is often associated with racial bias; however, a person can have a bias based on someone's gender, sexual orientation, intellectual and/or physical ability, culture, occupation, income, language, and other demographics. The University of California, San Francisco Office of Diversity and Outreach (2019) defines bias as:

> Prejudice in favor of or against one thing, person, or group compared with another usually in a way that's considered to be unfair. Biases may be held by an individual, group, or institution and can have negative or positive consequences. (para. 1)

There are different categories of bias: implicit and explicit. We tackle both implicit and explicit bias in Chapter 2; however, in this chapter, our core focus is on acknowledging unconscious bias. There are dozens of types of bias that exist. However, for our purposes in this book focused on culturally responsive teaching in person and online, Table 1.1 details five types of bias that are common. Please note that this list is not exhaustive. Additional information on why those five types of biases are particularly problematic within DELE is also shared in Table 1.1.

Table 1.1 ◆ Types of Bias

TYPE OF BIAS	OVERVIEW	WHY IS IT PROBLEMATIC?
Affinity	Favoring others who have the same perspectives, experiences, and background. As teachers, we may be kinder to students who come from the same neighborhoods as us or those whose parents attended the same college as us.	Teaching in diverse classrooms means that there may be a student whose parents did not attend college at all or who is not from the same or similar type of neighborhood. Giving certain students favor because of affinity bias will be unfair to the other students.
Confirmation	An unwillingness to take in new ideas and understandings; seeking out information that will support preconceived beliefs.	We all have unconscious biases that have shaped the way we think about issues. As we learn and receive new knowledge, confirmation bias can prohibit us from growing and using the newly learned knowledge to think about issues in other ways.

(Continued)

(Continued)

TYPE OF BIAS	OVERVIEW	WHY IS IT PROBLEMATIC?
Gender	Preferring one gender over others. Teachers may have different expectations for their male students, encouraging them to take an interest in STEM fields, while leading female students toward nursing and education. Female students may be encouraged to sit quietly while male students are rewarded for their outgoingness.	Part of teaching involves mentoring students and helping them leverage their own strengths to be successful in the future. If teachers are holding low expectations for their students because of their gender, or not recommending them for certain careers, then their future occupations, salary, and quality of life will be impacted.
Name	Avoiding people based on their names being perceived as different, difficult to pronounce, or too unique or against the norm.	The students may not get called on to answer questions because the teacher may be uncomfortable pronouncing their names. Teachers may not choose students based on their names to apply for competitive scholarships or be part of after-school clubs. When hiring students for internships and service-learning projects, those with more White American-sounding names may receive more callbacks.
Racial	Treatment of others based on their racial and ethnic backgrounds. As teachers, the way in which we speak to students, the knowledge we believe they bring to the classroom, and thoughts about their families and communities can all be impacted by racial biases that we may hold.	Racial bias can affect the way in which we discipline students. Pipeline to prison routes start at a very young age in early childhood education. We may call the police on Black and Latinx students after they are involved in a fight, whereas we may call the parents of White students for the same behaviors that the Black and Latinx exhibited by fighting. We may believe certain racial groups do not have higher education, and thus, it will be difficult for certain students to be successful in college preparatory programs.

ANTI-BIAS EXERCISE 1.1

Now that you have read about some of the different types of bias, think about how they could be present within education contexts and how they can affect the learning experiences of your students. Jot down your thoughts in the space provided below.

_____

_____

_____

Regardless of whether the bias is unconscious, the impact it can have on our students and their future is enormous. Watch this short, but powerful TED Talk Live video, on the impact that teacher bias can have on their students, from the students' perspective.

Scan this QR code to watch a TED Talks Live Short on unconscious bias.

WHAT UNCONSCIOUS BIAS "LOOKS" LIKE IN ONLINE AND IN-PERSON EDUCATION CONTEXTS

In both in-person and online classes alike, our unconscious bias is present in the ways that we teach and facilitate learning. An unconscious bias may also be known as an *implicit bias*. These are the types of biases that we unintentionally have. In Chapter 2, we get more into how to reduce implicit and explicit bias, but first we need to work through acknowledging our unconscious bias. Lavy and Sand (2018) found that, due to implicit biases related to gender, math teachers tend to call on boys more than they do girls. Similarly, Baker et al. (2018) found that online instructors were more likely to respond to discussion board posts submitted by White male students than all other student groups. Below, Table 1.2 provides examples of how unconscious bias can show up across learning contexts in the ways that we interact with students, develop lessons, discipline students, grade student work, and communicate with families. It is important to understand what unconscious bias *looks* like, as we continue our journey in recognizing it in our own actions, beliefs, and perspectives.

Table 1.2 • Examples of Unconscious Bias in In-Person and Online Learning Environments

UNCONSCIOUS BIAS	IN-PERSON LEARNING ENVIRONMENTS	ONLINE LEARNING ENVIRONMENTS
Interaction with students	When a boy who is significantly taller than the rest of the students walks into his seventh-grade classroom, the teacher thinks he is over 13 years of age and is repeating the school year, as opposed to having a taller than average height for his age.	After hearing the recorded accented greetings of the Latinx and Asian students in their first day of class discussion posting, the teacher surmises that she has a large number of English Language Learners in her class.
Lesson plan development	A teacher assumes that the Asian students in his class are Chinese and makes a concerted effort to integrate cultural content about and by Chinese authors. He later learns that his students are, in fact, Korean.	In a virtual small group activity, the teacher intentionally places the Black students in separate breakout rooms to keep them on task and not distract the other non-Black students.

(Continued)

(Continued)

UNCONSCIOUS BIAS	IN-PERSON LEARNING ENVIRONMENTS	ONLINE LEARNING ENVIRONMENTS
Student discipline	An interracial group of boys is disrupting the class, and the teacher singles out the only Black boy and sends him to the principal's office.	The teacher places a student who has an IEP for emotional disturbance in a separate breakout room to complete their work independently as punishment for making a joke and disrupting class.
Grading assignments	A teacher is surprised to receive a well-written paper by a Latinx student and wonders if they plagiarized his assignment.	A teacher uses online track changes to grade assignments by Black students, with greater scrutiny than White students in the class, highlighting simple errors that they do not highlight on their White students' papers.
Interacting with the families	A teacher asks an Iranian mother to participate on a panel about the immigrant experience and does not believe the mother when she explains that she is an American citizen.	A teacher concludes that a Native American mother does not care about her child's education because she is not available at home during the virtual school day to assist the student with classwork.

ANTI-BIAS EXERCISE 1.2

Stop and Reflect: Identify and reflect on an instance when your unconscious bias influenced your teaching. Jot down in the space below what the bias was and how you think it may have impacted your students.

_____

_____

_____

IMPACT OF BIAS ON TEACHING AND LEARNING

As teachers, we have a significant impact on the students entrusted to our care. Our unconscious biases shape the way that we see our students, what we believe about our students, and how we treat our students. Finnerty (2018) identified myriad of research studies that "identify the potential effects of unconscious bias when White teachers interact with Black boys" (p. 56) regarding how they look at the expectations of classroom behavior, perceptions of hostility and violence, assumptions of innocence and accountability, and expectations of intelligence and academic performance. For students of color, our actions based on our biases whether it be discipline referrals, letters of recommendations, or placement into special gifted programs, have a direct impact on their opportunities (Schwartz, 2019). Whether learning takes place in person or online, the impact of our unconscious biases play out within and extend beyond our classrooms. How we treat our students and the decisions we make concerning our students can influence what our students believe about themselves, shape their academic trajectories, and influence their life chances.

A substantial and growing body of research links teachers' unconscious bias in teaching and learning with student outcomes and life chances (Finnerty, 2018). For example, implicit bias about students' intelligence and capacity to learn shapes teachers' expectations for students' academic performance, how teachers engage students in class, and how teachers grade their assignments. If students do not achieve reading proficiency by fourth grade, their likelihood of academic achievement, successful completion of ninth grade, taking advanced math courses, and completion of high school are all greatly reduced. Teachers' early assessments of student learning determine how students are tracked in school, as well as their educational opportunities.

Unconscious bias has also been linked to the school-to-prison pipeline. For example, early childhood educators are more likely to interpret the behavior of children of color, particularly Black boys, with aggression. Boys of color are more likely to be disciplined, suspended, and expelled from daycare and preschool than other children (Gilliam et al., 2016). The same pattern continues in elementary and high school. Students of color are less likely to be seen as innocent children and more likely to be attributed a level of maturity and knowledge beyond their years and therefore punished more severely. They are more likely to be suspended and expelled from school. School infractions involving children of color are also more likely to involve the police. With the increased absences from school, students of color are less likely to read on grade level or finish high school.

Scan this QR code to watch Helen Turnbull's TEDx Talk titled "Inclusion, Exclusion, Illusion and Collusion."

After high school, young men of color are more likely to go to prison than to college.

Culturally responsive teaching can help mitigate the impact of unconscious bias on teaching and learning. It begins with teacher self-awareness and reflection. Let's stop here, scan the QR code, and take some time to watch this TEDx Talk by Helen Turnbull titled "Inclusion, Exclusion, Illusion and Collusion" to prepare for completing Anti-Bias Exercise 1.3.

ANTI-BIAS EXERCISE 1.3

In the "Inclusion, Exclusion, Illusion and Collusion" TEDx Talk, Turnbull discusses how unconscious bias and blind spots can undermine our efforts to be inclusive. She asserts that "[t]he unchallenged brain is not worth trusting." She closes the talk by asking us to consider what it is we do to exclude others, and what we could pay more attention to, in order to widen our ingroup. These lessons extend to our teaching and learning.

Use the space below to capture your thoughts as you watch the TedTalk.

_____

_____

_____

TEACHER SELF-AWARENESS AND REFLECTION

Culturally responsive teaching requires us to develop self-awareness and engage in self-reflection to acknowledge, identify, and address our unconscious biases. Gay (2018) contends that teachers need to perform "careful *self-analyses* of what they believe about the relationship among culture, ethnicity, and intellectual ability; the expectations they hold for their students from different ethnic groups; and how their beliefs and expectations are manifested in instructional behaviors" (p. 81, emphasis in original). Through increased self-awareness and critical reflection, we can mitigate the impact of our implicit biases on teaching and learning. Becoming more self-aware can improve our interactions with students and families. Increased self-awareness can help us identify and address our blind spots, such as colorblindness, and examine the unconscious biases that unwittingly influence how we (mis)understand and (mis)interpret our students and their families. In Anti-Bias Exercise 1.4, we look at why it is important to engage in self-awareness and critical self-reflection.

ANTI-BIAS EXERCISE 1.4

Let's spend time thinking about the importance of self-awareness and critical self-reflection for teachers and what potential impacts it can have on shaping our biases. Consider the biases you have already started to acknowledge and complete the following sentences.

1) Self-awareness means to _____

2) Critical self-reflection is the process of _____

3) It is important to engage in self-awareness and critical self-reflection because

_____

STIFLING STEREOTYPES

Stereotypes are those oversimplified ideas, thoughts, and beliefs about entire groups of people based on shared characteristics such as race or ethnicity, gender, sexual orientation, and family income. Research has shown that stereotypes and negative attitudes toward students based on their race are not only concerning, but also can create lower expectations for students, impacting their motivation to do well in school (Clark & Zygmunt, 2014).

In addition to the negative consequences of stereotyping our students, they also will have to deal with stereotype threats. Stereotype threat describes the situation in which there is a negative stereotype about a persons' group, and he or she is concerned about being judged or treated negatively on the basis of this stereotype (Spencer et al., 2016, p. 416). For example, "women's math performance is disrupted under threat not because of insufficient talent in women but because women feel threatened by the possibility that their performance will confirm the negative stereotype associated with their social group" (Tomasetto et al., 2011, p. 943).

For girls in school, a stereotype threat such as this may impact how well they do on STEM assessments because they will be consumed with the thought that poor performance on their individual assessment will be seen as a result of them being a female and not that they individually did not do well on the test. There are many different stereotypes that we may bring to the classroom. To stifle them, we must acknowledge what they are. Take a moment to engage in Anti-Bias Exercise 1.5.

ANTI-BIAS EXERCISE 1.5

Before we can work toward stifling stereotypes, we must acknowledge the stereotypes we may already have about our students, their families, and communities. In the space below, share stereotypes that you have and want to address. Remember, this book serves as your own personal action planner, and no one will see what you write unless you choose to share it. By being honest with ourselves, we can start thinking about students, their families, and communities based on their individual merits and qualities. An example is provided in the first box.

CATEGORY	STEREOTYPE
Gender	Boys are more hyperactive and will come to the classroom with more behavior issues than girls.
Race/Ethnicity	
Family Income	
Student's Neighborhood	

Thank you for being honest with yourself and sharing stereotypes that you may have about students. How do you feel about what you wrote above? Where do you feel those stereotypes developed from? What do you want to do to ensure that these stereotypes do not impact teaching and learning?

_____

_____

_____

WHAT'S NEXT?

Now that we have explored how to acknowledge the unconscious biases that we may unintentionally bring into the classroom, we can use our new understanding to work on stifling them. In the next chapter, we will focus more on the nuances specific to both implicit and explicit bias. We encourage you to explore the responsive resources scattered throughout the book which provide more examples of unconscious bias in education, as well as complete this chapter's culturally sustaining checklist and action plan.

REFLECTION QUESTIONS

You have worked through Chapter I and explored the importance of focusing on the unconscious bias that is learned through family, society, and life experiences that we unintentionally bring into educational settings. Take a few minutes to read through and reflect on the questions below. They may seem familiar because they are variations of the ones you completed prior to reading this chapter. Once you have recorded your responses, go back to the beginning of the chapter to see how your knowledge, awareness, and skills surrounding unconscious bias have expanded.

- How do I define unconscious bias?

- What stereotypes have I held about students based on their race/ethnicity, gender, or family income level?

- How has my own bias impacted teaching and learning?

- What did I learn from this chapter?

_____

_____

_____

_____

_____

Appendix 1.1

Culturally Sustaining Checklist: Addressing Unconscious Bias

On a scale of 1–4, please select how much you agree or disagree with the following statements:

1 = Strongly Disagree   2 = Disagree   3 = Agree   4 = Strongly Agree

ON A SCALE OF 1–4, INDICATE YOUR LEVEL OF AWARENESS.	AWARENESS	NOTES FOR FURTHER DEVELOPMENT:
	I am aware that teachers can have bias against students.	
	I am aware that unconscious bias should be acknowledged.	
	I am aware of my unconscious bias.	
ON A SCALE OF 1–4, INDICATE YOUR LEVEL OF KNOWLEDGE.	**KNOWLEDGE**	**NOTES FOR FURTHER DEVELOPMENT:**
	I know that stereotypes can be hurtful to students and families.	
	I understand that there are different types of bias.	
	I know the impact that self-reflection can have on addressing bias.	
ON A SCALE OF 1–4, INDICATE YOUR LEVEL OF SKILL.	**SKILLS**	**NOTES FOR FURTHER DEVELOPMENT:**
	I can state some of the stereotypes that I have about students, their families, and their communities.	
	I can effectively engage in self-reflection.	
	I can teach my students as individuals and not based on group stereotypes.	

Appendix 1.2

Action Plan: How will I work toward addressing my unconscious biases?

What are three actions you can take to use what you have learned in this chapter to address any unconscious bias that you may bring to the teaching and learning environments?

1.

2.

3.

What supports or information do you need to successfully complete the three actions you listed above?

1.

2.

3.

What challenges and barriers do you expect to be faced with in carrying out the three actions you listed above, and what ideas do you have for addressing them?

CHALLENGES/BARRIERS	IDEAS TO ADDRESS THEM
1.	
2.	
3.	

How do you expect your students to benefit from you taking the three actions listed above?

_____

_____

_____

Appendix 1.3   Responsive Resources

Scan the QR codes below to access the following resources as you continue to learn about acknowledging unconscious bias.

RESOURCE TYPE	TITLE	QR CODE
Article	"5 Things Educators Can Do to Address Bias in their School" *(NEA EdJustice)*	
Book	*Unconscious Bias in Schools: A Developmental Approach to Racism* by Tracey A. Benson and Sarah E. Fiarman (Harvard Education Press)	
Podcast	"Unconscious Bias in Schools with Dr. Tracey Benson" by the Center for Racial Equity in Education (CREED) (On The Margins Podcast)	
Video	"How to Check Your Unconscious Bias - Dr. Jennifer Eberhardt" (The Global Goals)	

CHAPTER TWO

Reducing Implicit Bias and Explicit Bias

REFLECTION QUESTIONS

Before delving into the chapter's contents, take a few minutes to work through the following reflection questions. There is space provided below for your responses. We revisit variations of these reflection questions at the end of the chapter.

- How do I define the difference between implicit bias and explicit bias?

- What influences my perception of my student's ability and capacity to learn?

- What strategies can I employ to address my implicit bias?

- What strategies can I employ to address my explicit bias?

- What do I hope to learn from this chapter?

_____

_____

_____

_____

_____

_____

_____

_____

IT STARTS WITH YOU

Surveys show that teachers enter the profession because they want to make a difference in the lives of children, and contribute to the greater good of society (Menzies et al., 2015; Ni & Rorrer, 2018). Despite these good intentions, the reality is that our implicit biases are at work. Staats (2015) insists:

> In education, the real-life implications of implicit biases can create invisible barriers to opportunity and achievement for some students—a stark contrast to the values and intentions of educators and administrators who dedicate their professional lives to their students' success. Thus, it is critical for educators to identify any discrepancies that may exist between their conscious ideals and unconscious associations so that they can mitigate the effects of those implicit biases, thereby improving student outcomes and allowing students to reach their full potential. (p. 33)

Acknowledging and owning our biases may be uncomfortable, but it is necessary if we are to reduce the impact of implicit and explicit biases to provide equitable access and opportunities to minoritized and marginalized students. In this chapter, we provide you with strategies, resources, and examples. You can use these tools to reduce implicit bias and explicit bias as you build your culturally responsive teaching skills within Dynamic Equitable Learning Environments (DELE) by:

- Describing the differences between implicit bias and explicit bias
- Understanding and having awareness of any implicit biases we may currently hold
- Exploring strategies for reducing implicit bias in teaching and learning settings
- Discussing ways to block explicit bias from entering in-person and online classrooms

As you read through the chapter, we hope that you not only come to a greater understanding of how implicit bias and explicit bias can impact different groups of students in your in-person and online classrooms, but also that you feel confident in having the knowledge, awareness, and skills needed to address it.

DIFFERENTIATING BETWEEN IMPLICIT BIAS AND EXPLICIT BIAS

As mentioned in Chapter 1, unconscious bias is what is considered an implicit bias. There is also explicit bias. A simple way to remember the difference between the two is that implicit bias is invisible to the person who has the bias whereas explicit bias is exposed and open. More formal and detailed definitions are presented in Table 2.1, to provide you with context to successfully differentiate between implicit bias and explicit bias.

Table 2.1 • Definitions of Implicit Bias and Explicit Bias

IMPLICIT BIAS	EXPLICIT BIAS
The Racial Equity Tools (2021) website describes implicit bias by stating: "Implicit bias, also known as hidden bias, refers to the numerous ways in which we organize patterns 'thus creating real-world implications.' Exposure to structural and cultural racism has enabled stereotypes and biases to penetrate deep into our psyches. Implicit bias is one part of the system of inequity that serves to justify racist policies, practices and behaviors that persist in the mainstream culture and narratives" (para. 1).	The National Center for Cultural Competence at Georgetown University (2021) describes explicit bias by stating: "In the case of explicit or conscious [bias], the person is very clear about his or her feelings and attitudes, and related behaviors are conducted with intent. This type of bias is processed neurologically at a conscious level as declarative, semantic memory, and in words" (para. 1).

You now have a shorter description and a more detailed definition of both implicit bias and explicit bias. Sometimes it is helpful to hear examples, too. Scan the QR code to watch and listen to this short video titled "Implicit Bias vs Explicit Bias: What's the Difference?" that effectively, yet succinctly explains the differences between implicit bias and explicit bias.

Scan this QR code to watch a short video titled "Implicit Bias vs. Explicit Bias: What's the DIfference?"

STRATEGIES FOR REDUCING IMPLICIT BIAS IN TEACHING AND LEARNING

In the previous chapter, we learned about implicit bias, what it looks like across learning contexts, and its impact on teaching and learning. Here, we learn about five strategies to reduce implicit bias in teaching and learning: (1) take an implicit bias test, (2) become a reflective practitioner through journaling, (3) develop empathy, (4) collect data of teaching practices, and (5) use grading rubrics. While not exhaustive, these strategies will help make you more aware of your implicit biases and provide you with tools to minimize the impact on student learning.

#1: Take an Implicit Bias Test

To reduce your implicit bias, you need to first acknowledge and understand it. This can be accomplished by taking an implicit bias test. Project Implicit (2011) offers the Implicit Association Test (IAT), which:

> measures the strength of associations between concepts (e.g., Black people, gay people) and evaluations (e.g., good, bad) or

stereotypes (e.g., athletic, clumsy). The main idea is that making a response is easier when closely related items share the same response key. (para. 1)

See Anti-Bias Exercise 2.1 to take the test and reflect on what you learned about your implicit biases.

ANTI-BIAS EXERCISE 2.1

After reviewing the instructions and disclosures, take the following implicit bias test from Harvard University and Project Implicit by scanning the QR code.

What did you learn about your implicit biases?

_____

_____

_____

#2: Become a Reflective Practitioner by Keeping a Journal

Engaging in critical self-reflection by keeping a journal can help raise your self-awareness about how your implicit biases are influencing teaching and learning in both in-person and online classes. There are a number of different ways that you can prompt your regular self-reflection, for example:

- **Reflect on a specific exchange or encounter in class.** Describe what happened. What could you have done differently? What can you do to prepare for the next time a similar encounter occurs?

- **Reflect on a specific student in the class.** What are your perceptions of the student? What are your expectations for the student's success? What are the sources of your perceptions and expectations?

- **Consider your students' perspectives.** If your students were to describe you, what would they say? Would the students of color in your class agree? Would the female students in your class concur? Why do you think these would be their perspectives on you and your teaching? What can you do to learn and grow?

These are just a few examples of prompts that you can use to initiate your self-reflection. Such reflection activities are important to promote greater self-awareness. See Anti-Bias Exercise 2.2 for additional insight on how you can recognize and address your implicit bias.

ANTI-BIAS EXERCISE 2.2

Scan the QR code to watch this TedTalk by Jennefer Witter, "How Prejudiced Are You? Recognizing and Combating Unconscious Bias."

Record your initial responses to the TEDTalk and consider the implications for your first impressions of your students.

_____

_____

_____

#3: Develop Empathy

Implicit bias is rooted in limited experience with and understanding of people who you perceive to be different; they do not read as part of your in-group. Empathy—the ability to understand another's perspective and emotions; in other words, to walk in someone else's shoes—has been shown to reduce implicit bias and its impact on teaching and learning (Okonofua et al., 2016; Whitford & Emerson, 2019). Suttie (2016) recommends that teachers develop empathy for their students by learning about students' lives. Empathy should be enduring and inform how you relate to your students. See Anti-bias Exercise 2.3 to work through potential approaches that can be leveraged to develop empathy for your students.

ANTI-BIAS EXERCISE 2.3

Choose one of these five approaches to develop empathy for your students by learning more about them:

1. Ask students to complete a picture or diagram of their family, friends, and other people who are important in their lives (depending on age level).

2. Have lunch with one of your students.

3. Interview one of your student's parents/caregivers.

4. Conduct a home visit, in person or virtually.

5. Conduct a community walk or a virtual tour of a community agency.

After you complete one (or more) of these activities, record your experience and reflections here.

_____

_____

_____

#4: Collect Data on Your Everyday Teaching Practices

Is it possible that you are calling on your students who come from a higher socioeconomic background more than your students who come from a lower socioeconomic background?

Is it possible that you are grading the girls differently than you grade the boys?

Is it possible that you are more likely to identify when a student of color is misbehaving than you are when a White student is misbehaving?

While we may want to believe that we do not engage in such teaching practices, without data, it is difficult to be sure. To identify and address your implicit biases, you are encouraged to collect data on your teaching practices. Staats (2015) elaborates, "gathering meaningful data can bring to light trends and patterns in disparate treatment of individuals and throughout an institution that may otherwise go unnoticed" (p. 33). Staats continues, "doing so, of course, is easier said than done, given that educators are constantly pressed for time, face myriad challenges, and need crucial support from administrators to effectively manage student behavior" (p. 33).

To assist with data collection, Shah et al. (2021) developed a tool called EQUIP (Equity Quantified in Participation). EQUIP is "a customizable observation tool for tracking patterns in student participation" (para. 1), and can be used in real-time observations or with video recordings. EQUIP generates analytics of the number of times a student participates and the number of opportunities that an instructor makes available for students to engage. Such data is an integral part of teacher reflection and can help to shape teaching practices in Dynamic Equitable Learning Environments.

Scan this QR code to visit the EQUIP website.

Teachers can also request student data for careful analysis of the influence of implicit bias. For example, student discipline data might be revealing and could bring about shifts in thinking and behavior. Similarly, careful consideration of differences in students' academic achievement might also inspire deeper reflection on the influence of implicit biases and how such biases can be addressed and adjusted. By taking greater responsibility for the roles we play as teachers, we can unveil and unpack how our implicit biases may be influencing student learning. See Anti-bias Exercise 2.4 for guidance on how to more closely examine explicit bias in your teaching practice.

ANTI-BIAS EXERCISE 2.4

Choose an area of your teaching that you would like to more closely examine for the influence of implicit bias, for example, participation or discipline. For one week, keep a daily tally of which students participate in class, how often, and who does not. Or keep a daily tally of which students are disciplined, the nature of the infraction, the severity of the punishment, and who is not disciplined. At the end of the week, carefully analyze the data to identify patterns and omissions. Reflect on which implicit biases that you might see at work in the data, and consider how you might go about addressing this.

#5: Use Grading Rubrics

Assessment is also a place where the influence of implicit bias is evident. Quinn (2020) conducted a study to examine the influence of implicit racial bias on a third-grade writing sample that was essentially the same except the students' names were different. He found teachers were likely to grade the student with a name that signaled White more leniently than a student with a name that signaled Black. Quinn (2020) conducted the same experiment using a rubric and determined that the teacher's implicit bias decreased when grading the writing assignment. To address the impact of implicit bias on grading, consider removing the students' names and using a discrete rubric with a few direct criteria to assess student learning.

IDENTIFYING EXPLICIT BIAS IN TEACHING AND LEARNING

Thus far in Chapter 2, we have focused on strategies to reduce the impact of implicit bias in teaching and learning across contexts. Now, we turn our attention to explicit bias. Explicit bias is the traditional form of bias, when people are fully conscious and aware of their attitudes and beliefs about a person or group. Annamma and Morrison (2018) caution that the current trend toward implicit bias should not overlook teachers who subscribe to overtly racist beliefs that create hostile learning environments. In Table 2.2, we provide examples of explicit bias in in-person and online learning contexts.

Table 2.2 • Examples of Explicit Bias in In-Person and Online Learning Environments

EXPLICIT BIAS	IN-PERSON LEARNING ENVIRONMENTS	ONLINE LEARNING ENVIRONMENTS
Interaction with students	A teacher compliments a Latinx student, telling him that he is different from his classmates and that she sees him doing great things in his life.	A teacher insists that the English Language Learners write in the chat in English, thereby limiting the students' learning and participation in class.
Lesson plan development	A teacher creates word problems for a math test based on slavery and the Underground Railroad, for example, how many miles could eight slaves travel in 1 hour?	When a student posts a complaint in the online "water cooler" area that the history class does not cover women's contributions, the teacher counters with a typed response to the class that women did not win wars.
Student discipline	In an outburst, a teacher tells a student who regularly causes disruptions in her class that he will never amount to anything more than the men in front of the liquor store that she passes every day on her way to school.	A teacher removes a student by placing them in a virtual "waiting room" during a live online class session, as an equivalent of sitting in the hallway after they make a disruptive comment for the second time.

EXPLICIT BIAS	IN-PERSON LEARNING ENVIRONMENTS	ONLINE LEARNING ENVIRONMENTS
Grading assignments	A teacher lowers her expectations of an Indigenous student's performance on an exam because they believe this is the best that the student can do.	A teacher tells a colleague, "I match the student's learning management system's online profile picture with their 'ethnic' name, and I already know they are going to struggle in my class."
Interacting with the families	A teacher asks a colleague to attend a parent-teacher conference with her because she is afraid a Black mother is going to be very aggressive and she wants a witness in her defense.	Frustrated by a students' weak internet connection, a teacher questions parents' priorities when they see a large flat-screen television in the background of the student's Zoom meetings instead of paying for a more expensive internet service that would provide the student with a higher bandwidth and faster connection.

BLOCKING EXPLICIT BIAS IN TEACHING AND LEARNING

Here, we focus on four strategies to block explicit bias in teaching and learning: (1) making yourself uncomfortable; (2) educating yourself on history and sociopolitical context; (3) understanding the sociopolitical consequences of racism; and (4) moving beyond reflection to raise critical consciousness. While not exhaustive, these strategies will help you mitigate the influence of explicit biases in your teaching and learning.

Make Yourself Uncomfortable: To challenge and disrupt our explicit biases, we must make ourselves uncomfortable. This entails placing ourselves in unfamiliar settings where we are in the minority. This might include visiting a new place of worship or attending an event in a new neighborhood. Such cross-cultural experiences challenge our assumptions, disrupt our biases, and offer counternarratives to the stories we tell ourselves about people who are different from us.

Educate Yourself on History and Influences on the Sociopolitical Context in Which Your Students Live: Our explicit biases are often rooted in a lack of knowledge and understanding about history. The omitted stories of minoritized and marginalized communities contribute to the stereotypes about their populations. By understanding history from their perspectives, new interpretations and understandings of the groups and of ourselves can emerge. Such education can take place by reading history books written by scholars of color and watching documentaries that tell a more complete and complex story of human history.

Understand the Sociopolitical Consequences of Racism and Discrimination on Students: With an evolved understanding of history, we can develop an understanding of the sociopolitical forces shaping our current context, particularly the context shaping our students' lived experiences. Such an understanding is key to culturally responsive pedagogy. For example, Ladson-Billings (2014) emphasized the importance of teachers' acknowledgment of the sociopolitical ramifications of race and culture, as well as their recognition of how racism and discrimination impact students. With a keen understanding of the sociopolitical context, explicit biases about the deficits of the marginalized status of certain communities will be challenged and dismantled.

Move Beyond Reflection to Raise Your Critical Consciousness: Reflection is a place for educators to start but not to end their efforts to address their biases. To eliminate explicit biases, it is important to understand how such biases are connected to and reinforced by structural inequities in schools. Advancing reflection to raise critical consciousness will call into question explicit biases and interrogate the underlying assumptions. Annamma and Morrison (2018) assert:

> We extend this critical consciousness raising to explicitly address racism; this conscious raising must explicitly consider racism's intersections with other marginalizing oppressions, both in the classroom and society. For educators to engage in a radical critique, they must understand how societal inequities are (re)produced . . . and how shifts in their own consciousness and understanding of learning can disrupt intersectional injustices. (p. 123)

Developing critical consciousness will not only enable a teacher to disrupt their own explicit biases, but also to develop a needed critique of intersecting inequities and injustices taking place in schools and society.

ANTI-BIAS EXERCISE 2.5

To address your explicit bias, educate yourself by engaging with critical essays, podcasts, and other programming. For example, watch the *13th* by Ava DuVernay or read Chris Collins' essay, "What Is White Privilege, Really?" There are ample equity and social justice educational resources available. Choose one such resource, and use the space below to reflect on how what you learned challenged your thinking and understanding.

_____

_____

_____

WHAT'S NEXT?

We hope that you feel more confident in your understanding of implicit bias and explicit bias and how they impact in-person and online teaching and learning environments. Regardless of the prevalence of implicit bias and explicit bias, as culturally responsive teachers, we can reduce bias in our classrooms and strengthen the DELE that we are crafting with our students. Before you go on to Chapter 3, which is focused on eliminating microaggressions, revisit the reflection questions below to see how your thinking around implicit bias and explicit bias has changed. Also, complete this chapter's culturally sustaining checklist and action plan.

REFLECTION QUESTIONS

You have worked through Chapter 2 and explored the importance of reducing both implicit and explicit bias in in-person and online teaching and learning environments. Take a few minutes to read through and reflect on the questions below. They may seem familiar because they are variations of the ones you completed prior to reading this chapter. Once you have recorded your responses, go back to the beginning of the chapter to see how your knowledge, awareness, and skills surrounding implicit and explicit bias have expanded.

(Continued)

(Continued)

- How do I define the difference between implicit bias and explicit bias?

- What influences my perception of my student's ability and capacity to learn?

- What strategies can I employ to address my implicit bias?

- What strategies can I employ to address my explicit bias?

- What did I learn from this chapter?

_____

_____

_____

_____

_____

_____

_____

_____

_____

_____

_____

_____

_____

_____

Appendix 2.1

Culturally Sustaining Checklist: Addressing Unconscious Bias

On a scale of 1–4, please select how much you agree or disagree with the following statements.

| 1 = Strongly Disagree | 2 = Disagree | 3 = Agree | 4 = Strongly Agree |

ON A SCALE OF 1–4, INDICATE YOUR LEVEL OF AWARENESS.	AWARENESS	NOTES FOR FURTHER DEVELOPMENT:
	I am aware that teachers' bias can be either implicit or explicit.	
	I am aware that implicit bias is unintentional.	
	I am aware that explicit bias is intentional.	
ON A SCALE OF 1–4, INDICATE YOUR LEVEL OF KNOWLEDGE.	**KNOWLEDGE**	**NOTES FOR FURTHER DEVELOPMENT:**
	I know the difference between implicit and explicit bias.	
	I know that implicit bias can be hurtful to students and families.	
	I know that explicit bias contributes to racism.	
ON A SCALE OF 1–4, INDICATE YOUR LEVEL OF SKILL.	**SKILLS**	**NOTES FOR FURTHER DEVELOPMENT:**
	I can identify instances of implicit bias.	
	I can identify instances of explicit bias.	
	I can conduct self-awareness techniques to reduce instances of implicit and explicit bias.	

Appendix 2.2

Action Plan: How will I work toward reducing implicit and explicit biases?

What are three actions you can take to use what you have learned in this chapter to reduce implicit bias and/or explicit bias within in-person and online teaching and learning environments?

I.

2.

3.

What supports or information do you need to successfully complete the three actions you listed above?

I.

2.

3.

What challenges and barriers do you expect to be faced with in carrying out the three actions you listed above, and what ideas do you have for addressing them?

CHALLENGES/BARRIERS	IDEAS TO ADDRESS THEM
I.	
2.	
3.	

How do you expect your students to benefit from you taking the three actions listed above?

_____

_____

_____

Appendix 2.3   Responsive Resources

Scan the QR codes below to access the following resources as you continue to learn about reducing implicit bias and explicit bias.

RESOURCE TYPE	TITLE	URL
Article	"Teacher Bias: The Elephant in the Classroom" *(The Graide Network)*	
Book	*Implicit Bias in Schools: A Practitioner's Guide* by Gina Laura Gullo, Kelly Capatosto, and Cheryl Staats (Routledge)	
Podcast	"Implicit Bias with Mahzarin Banaji" (Opinion Science)	
Video	"When Implicit Bias Becomes Explicit | Megan Fuciarelli" (TEDx Talks)	

CHAPTER THREE

Eliminating Microaggressions

REFLECTION QUESTIONS

Before delving into the chapter's contents, take a few minutes to work through the following reflection questions. There is space provided below for your responses. We revisit variations of these reflection questions at the end of the chapter.

- To my understanding, what is a microaggression?
- How can microaggressions impact the classroom environment?
- What is the difference between a microassault, microinsult, and microinvalidation?
- What do I hope to learn from this chapter?

_____

_____

_____

_____

_____

_____

_____

_____

SO *WHAT* IS A "MICROAGGRESSION" AND *HOW* IS IT CONNECTED TO CULTURALLY RESPONSIVE TEACHING?

The third and final chapter of Part I of this book is focused on microaggressions. The term *microaggressions* was coined by Harvard professor Chester Pierce in 1978 to describe the subtle, and sometimes nonverbal, exchanges that have offensive undertones toward persons of color. Many researchers have added to it over the last few decades (Ong & Burrow, 2017). For this book, we are using the definition by Sue (2010) who describes microaggressions as "everyday verbal, nonverbal, and environmental slights, snubs, or insults, whether intentional or unintentional, that communicate hostile, derogatory, or negative messages to target persons based solely upon their marginalized group membership" (p. 8). In addition to microaggressions targeted at racial minorities, microaggressions can also be directed toward other marginalized groups including women, people within the LGBTQ community, and persons with disabilities.

What makes microaggressions so harmful is that the language that is said is not always seen as overly offensive. However, the undertones within microaggressions can have dangerous, racist, and sexist messages. Culturally responsive teaching encompasses the spirit of valuing and affirming all students and brings in the perspectives, ideas, and lived experiences of students in the classroom to inform the way they learn. When we inadvertently use microaggressions in the language we use in schools, it goes against the pedagogical structure of culturally responsive teaching. To create, nurture, and maintain Dynamic Equitable Learning Environments (DELE), they must be free from microaggressions. Similar to how we learned about acknowledging the bias that we may bring into the classroom in Chapters 1 and 2, we may not even be aware that the statements we say and the language we use in both in-person and online learning environments are, in fact, types of microaggressions. This is why this chapter is so important to our growth and development as culturally responsive teachers.

In this chapter, we provide you with information surrounding microaggressions to prepare you in ensuring that the DELE you teach in are free from them by:

- Identifying the different types of microaggressions

- Describing the ways in which microassaults, microinsults, and microinvalidations can be delivered within in-person and online learning environments

- Discerning the harmful nature that microaggressions can have on students' ability to have positive schooling experiences

- Demonstrating ways that teachers can use microresistance and microinterventions to eliminate microaggressions

As you go through the chapter, please remember to come to the content with an open mind and bring a willingness to be truthful and reflective of your past experiences, to make a positive impact on future interactions and exchanges with your students.

MOVING TOWARD MITIGATING MICROAGGRESSIONS

To work on eliminating the microaggressions that are present in teaching and learning environments, we must not only be aware of what a microaggression is, but also how they are delivered and what different types of microaggressions exist. Microaggressions can be communicated within curriculum and instruction which can have harmful impacts on minoritized and marginalized groups of students (Sue et al., 2019). Remember, microaggressions by definition are subtle, and can be ingrained into a teacher's everyday language without them realizing it. For example, although seemingly harmless, mispronouncing students' names are microaggressions that actually support racism in schools (Kohli & Solórzano, 2012). Many of the students whose names are mispronounced are students of color. While it may seem like an innocent mistake to teachers, the impact of having your culturally diverse name mispronounced over and over again by your teachers can be quite harmful to the student's psychological well-being.

Sue et al. (2007) describes three types of microaggressions: (1) microassault, (2) microinsult, and (3) microinvalidation.

Microassault: "An explicit racial derogation characterized primarily by a verbal or nonverbal attack meant to hurt the intended victim through name-calling, avoidant behavior, or purposeful discriminatory actions" (Sue et al., 2007, p. 274). Think of a microassault as believing that a person is more of an exception to a well-known stereotype about the demographic group they are part of.

Example: "You are well informed about scientific topics for a girl."

Microinsult: "Communications that convey rudeness and insensitivity and demean a person's racial heritage or identity. Microinsults represent subtle snubs, frequently unknown to the perpetrator, but clearly convey a hidden insulting message to the recipient of color" (Sue et al., 2007, p. 274). Think of a microinsult as a comment that offends the receiver but the giver of the comment actually thinks it is a compliment.

Example: "Are you sure your father is an anthropologist? I thought all Mexicans were farmers."

Microinvalidation: "Communications that exclude, negate, or nullify the psychological thoughts, feelings, or experiential reality of a person of color" (Sue et al., 2007, p. 274). Think of microinvalidation as not taking into account the experiences that marginalized groups experience daily, because of their race, class, gender, and/or sexual orientation.

Example: "It's a shame that Black students are only accepted into Ivy League colleges because of affirmative action."

The examples provided above of the different types of microaggressions are just a few different statements that can be subtly, yet harmfully communicated to students. Table 3.1 provides examples of microaggressions that could be present in both in-person and online learning settings.

Table 3.1 • Examples of Microaggressions in In-Person and Online Learning Settings

TYPE OF MICROAGGRESSION	IN-PERSON LEARNING SETTING	ONLINE LEARNING SETTING
Microassault	During small group work, the teacher tells a Latinx student **"make sure you speak in English"** to imply that they are an English Language Learner who should accommodate their classmates whose native language is English, or assuming that they do not speak English well enough to contribute to the small group work.	During a live synchronous class debate, the teacher reminds the female Black students to **"not be so aggressive in their responses"** to imply that Black females are more aggressive whereas White females are seen as assertive.
Microinsults	During a social studies lesson focused on neighborhoods and community responsibilities, a Turkish student responds that they are from the neighborhood near the school, and the teacher responds **"but where are you *really* from,"** implying that they were not born in the same country that the school was located.	In an online breakout room, the teacher asks the group of students, "Who typed the notes appearing on the screen share?" When the teacher learns that a Black student was the note taker, they respond **"Interesting! This is actually written using proper English"** to imply their surprise that the student did not write using Black Vernacular English (also known as Ebonics).

TYPE OF MICROAGGRESSION	IN-PERSON LEARNING SETTING	ONLINE LEARNING SETTING
Microinvalidation	A teacher tells her classroom that they will not be participating in the district's annual cultural festival since **"everyone is part of the same human race,"** implying that the unique experiences of students based on their cultures are not necessary and should not be recognized.	A teacher is upset that their school district leadership is requiring each teacher to identify the needs of students from low-income families during virtual learning. She says to another teacher, **"People need to work hard, like my ancestors did, instead of asking for handouts,"** implying that everyone had equitable opportunities toward upward mobility and not acknowledging the centuries of racism and discrimination that previously and currently exist.

These are just a few examples of microaggressions that may be present in either in-person or online learning environments. Scan this QR code that will take you to an article on The Evocate website that lists 33 microaggressions that educators commit daily.

Scan this QR code to read the article "33 Microaggressions That Educators Commit Daily" from The Edvocate.

ANTI-BIAS EXERCISE 3.1

Table 3.1 illustrated just a few microaggressions that may be present in in-person and online learning environments. Can you think of one example of a microassault, microinsult, and microinvalidation you have witnessed or even inadvertently said yourself? This could have been said to students, their families, and even colleagues.

TYPE OF MICROAGGRESSION	MICROASSAULT	MICROINSULT	MICROINVALIDATION
Describe the microaggression and what was said.			
Who said the microaggression?			
Who was the microaggression directed toward?			
Was the microaggression said in an in-person or online learning environment?			

MICROAGGRESSIONS IN VIRTUAL ENVIRONMENTS

The presence of microaggressions is not restricted to in-person learning environments (Ortega et al., 2018). In fact, while issues with equitable access to the internet, fatigue, and varied home life backgrounds while using online conferencing through tools such as Zoom have been documented, the prevalence of microaggressions in these spaces has not (Cheung et al., 2021). Online blog postings can also have different forms of microaggressions including microinsults, microassaults, and microinvalidations (Clark et al., 2011). As more and more learning continues to take place in virtual environments, the use of microaggressions in these spaces must be considered. Anti-Bias Exercise 3.2 provides you the space to get started.

ANTI-BIAS EXERCISE 3.2

Stop and reflect here. As you have read, microaggressions can happen in online forums. What are some reasons why people feel comfortable in delivering microaggressions in online environments?

_____

_____

_____

The Online Network of Educators (@ONE) (Torres, 2018) suggests establishing netiquette guidelines within online classes that are anti-microaggression. This means that, early on, students and teachers are aware of the language and behaviors that should be displayed during online teaching and learning. Since microaggressions are so subtle, and many times inadvertently and unknowingly delivered, having anti-microaggression netiquette expectations can serve as a helpful reminder to the class community and is an integral part of culturally responsive teaching.

MAXIMIZING MICRORESISTENCE

Despite the prevalence of microaggressions in in-person and online learning environments, there are many ways that we can support all students, and collectively co-construct DELE that are free from microaggressions. As teachers, we can use our position and power in microresistance efforts through microinterventions, which are:

> the everyday words or deeds, whether intentional or unintentional, that communicates to targets of microaggressions (a) validation of their experiential reality, (b) value as a person, (c) affirmation of their racial or group identity, (d) support and encouragement, and (e) reassurance that they are not alone. (Sue et al., 2019, p. 134)

Instead of using language that assaults, insults, and invalidates our students, we can instead make sure students know that their lived experiences matter; provide opportunities for students to authentically contribute their ideas, values, and beliefs to the class; nurture and help students develop holistically; and provide an environment that is filled with reciprocity and community. Acts of microresistance can take place in person and online. Research has shown that online forums present a space where persons of color can resist and call out microaggressions (Eschmann, 2021). Here are three examples of ways to be microresistant to microaggressions:

- **Microaffirmations** (Rowe, 2008): One way to be microresistant to microaggressions is to counter a microaggression with a microaffirmation. Microaffirmations are "tiny acts of opening doors of opportunity, gestures of inclusion and caring, and graceful acts of listening" (p. 46). We can provide microaffirmations to our students by publicly and proudly affirming and appreciating the contributions they bring to the classroom. Microaffirmations allow us to counteract instances of microinsults and microassaults.

- **Perception Checking** (Cheung et al., 2021): As a bystander, and even sometimes as an offender, you may notice discomfort in the person who received a microaggression. You can check in with the person and ask, for example, "Sanaya, did you just feel dismissed by the comment Jen made? It seemed dismissive to me. If so, are you okay if I say something?" (para. 14). If you were the one who inadvertently delivered the microaggression, you can ask the person who received it, "Kim, I think I just insulted your performance based on stereotypes. I apologize and would like to work on that. I am truly sorry, Kim." Perception checking, as a form of microresistance, acknowledges that a microaggression was delivered and takes action to eliminate them in the future.

- **Educate the Offender** (Sue et al., 2019): Part of the aim of microinterventions is to educate the person who is delivering the microaggression. In this case, the person is known as the offender. The offender can be you, a colleague, or even a student. To be microresistent to microaggressions, we must educate the offender to let them know that their words are microaggressive, harmful, and not appropriate in school settings.

Table 3.2 provides examples of acts of microresistance and microinterventions by providing microaffirmations, perception checking, and educating the offender in in-person and online learning environments.

Table 3.2 • Acts of Microresistance and Microintervention in In-Person and Online Learning Environments

ACT OF MICRORESISTANCE AND MICROINTERVENTION	IN-PERSON	ONLINE
Providing microaffirmations	A student shares a family tradition that is associated with a religious holiday that is not well known in the country that the school is located in. Another student looks confused and uninterested in their classmate's cultural sharing. The teacher verbally thanks the student for sharing and connects what the student shared to the larger lesson, ensuring that the other students in the class understand the importance of their classmate's contribution and that the student who shared knows their cultural traditions matter.	A student presents an online slideshow of artwork that is special to their culture during a synchronous lesson. As the student presents, another classmate uses disparaging language to describe the images on the slideshow. As the teacher, you immediately intercede and remind all students that we all bring in special pieces of our culture to the classroom community that make the school community so special.
Perception checking	At lunchtime, a group of students are discussing sports. There are a few female students at the table. When one of the female students tries to engage in the discussion, they are dismissed by one of the male students who states that they are a girl so she does not really	During a virtual science lab peer simulation, a student tells you as the teacher that their peer, who identifies as a gay male, may be too scared and weak to lead the experiments. The peer is present for the exchange. Not only do you educate the offender, but you

ACT OF MICRORESISTANCE AND MICROINTERVENTION	IN-PERSON	ONLINE
	know sports. You as the teacher can perception check with the female student, acknowledge their dismissal, and ask the student if they are comfortable with you addressing it with the student who delivered the microaggression.	also engage in perception checking with the student who received the microaggression.
Educate the offender	During a grade partner meeting, your colleague is speaking about another student using a microinvalidation, stating that the student is only in the gifted program because a diversity quota needed to be filled. You immediately explain to the colleague that in fact the student held the appropriate academic credentials to qualify for the gifted program and you explain that their statement is a form of a microaggression.	Your students were required to submit responses to questions on the online discussion board. You see that some students' postings included microaggressions. You take screenshots and review the responses with the students who used microaggressions to show them how their language changes when speaking to different students whose demographics may be different than theirs.

ANTI-BIAS EXERCISE 3.3

We hope that you will choose to engage in acts of microresistance and use microintervention as part of your path toward culturally responsive teaching. Let's take some time to think about what are some of the first steps. You can use your notes here as a springboard when you complete the Action Plan at the end of this chapter. Complete the following sentences.

I can provide microaffirmations to my students during in-person learning by

_____

(Continued)

(Continued)

I can conduct perception checking during online learning instruction by

_____

I can educate a student or colleague when they have delivered a microaggression in either an online and in-person learning environment by

_____

MODELS TO MOVE BEYOND MICROAGGRESSIONS

In addition to being microresistant to microaggressions and using microinterventions to call out and minimize the use of microinsults, microassaults, and microinvalidations in in-person and online learning spaces, there are additional models and frameworks that can be useful. These include Open the Front Door (OTFD), ACTION, and GRIT (Gather, Restate, Inquire, Talk it Out). Table 3.3 provides a brief overview of each of the models and highlights the different components of each. As you read through them, think about which one you may connect with more. Or one that you think you would feel comfortable using when faced with microaggressions within your school district, school, or classroom.

Table 3.3 • Microresistance Models

OTFD is a communication model with four parts that can be used to address and talk through the presence of microaggressions (Learning Forum, 2016).	**O**bserve: The objective and observable facts. **T**hink: Thoughts as a result of observations. **F**eel: Feelings and/or emotions that are a result of the observation. **D**esire: Share the desired outcome statement.

ACTION is an acronym that serves as a guide and spells out the steps that a person can take when faced with a microaggression, as opposed to doing nothing (Cheung et al., 2016).	**A**sk clarifying questions to assist with understanding intentions. **C**ome from curiosity, not judgment. **T**ell what you observed as problematic in a factual manner. **I**mpact exploration: ask for, and/or state, the potential impact of such a statement or action on others. **O**wn your own thoughts and feelings around the impact. **N**ext steps: Request appropriate action to be taken.
GRIT (Warner et al., 2019) is a mnemonic method that can be used to address microaggressions in a way that is non-accusatory.	**G**ather your thoughts. **R**estate. **I**nquire. **T**alk it out.

Any of the models in Table 3.3 can be used as a starting point in addressing microaggressions. Sometimes, it is helpful to have a guide and language to lean on when having these uncomfortable, but necessary conversations. As we continue to cover related topics in this book, you will see how when taken together, we strengthen the knowledge, awareness, and skills needed to be a culturally responsive teacher.

WHAT'S NEXT?

We hope that you have a better understanding of what microaggressions are, the types of microaggressions that exist, and how they can impact teaching and learning. Now that you have spent time acknowledging unconscious bias, thought of ways to reduce implicit and explicit bias, as well as how to use microresistance and microintervention efforts to eliminate microaggressions, we can move on to Part II of this book, which is focused on co-constructing meaningful connections with students and their families. Before you move on to Part II, complete the reflection questions below to see how your thinking has changed around microaggressions and use this chapter's culturally sustaining checklist and action plan to support your plan for incorporating the content in this chapter within your culturally responsive teaching practices.

REFLECTION QUESTIONS

You have worked through Chapter 3 and explored ways to eliminate microaggressions within in-person and online learning environments. Take a few minutes to read through and reflect on the reflection questions below. They may seem familiar because they are variations of the ones you completed prior to reading this chapter. Once you have recorded your responses, go back to the beginning of the chapter to see how your knowledge, awareness, and skills surrounding microaggressions have expanded.

- What is a microaggression?

- In what ways can microassaults, microinsults, and microinvalidations impact in-person and online learning environments?

- How can I maximize microresistance?

- What did I learn from this chapter?

_____

_____

_____

_____

_____

_____

_____

_____

_____

_____

Appendix 3.1

Culturally Sustaining Checklist: Mitigating Microaggressions

On a scale of I–4, please select how much you agree or disagree with the following statements.

I = Strongly Disagree   2 = Disagree   3 = Agree   4 = Strongly Agree

ON A SCALE OF I–4, INDICATE YOUR LEVEL OF AWARENESS.	AWARENESS	NOTES FOR FURTHER DEVELOPMENT:
	I am aware of what a microaggression is.	
	I am aware that there are different types of microaggressions.	
	I am aware of how microaggressions can impact educational experiences for students.	
ON A SCALE OF I–4, INDICATE YOUR LEVEL OF KNOWLEDGE.	**KNOWLEDGE**	**NOTES FOR FURTHER DEVELOPMENT:**
	I know the definitions of different types of microaggressions.	
	I know how each type of microaggression can impact teaching and learning.	
	I know the value of using microresistance to address microaggressions in the classroom.	
ON A SCALE OF I–4, INDICATE YOUR LEVEL OF SKILL.	**SKILLS**	**NOTES FOR FURTHER DEVELOPMENT:**
	I can articulate to colleagues the danger of microaggressions in education.	
	I can provide an example of each type of microaggression in in-person and online learning environments.	
	I can maximize my own microresistance efforts.	

Appendix 3.2

Action Plan: How Will I Work Toward Eliminating
Microaggressions in My Classroom and School Community?

What are three actions you can take to use what you have learned in this chapter to address the presence of microaggressions that may present in your classroom and school community?

1.

2.

3.

What supports or information do you need to successfully complete the three actions you listed above?

1.

2.

3.

What challenges and barriers do you expect to be faced with in carrying out the three actions you listed above, and what ideas do you have for addressing them?

CHALLENGES/BARRIERS	IDEAS TO ADDRESS THEM
1.	
2.	
3.	

How do you expect your students to benefit from you taking the three actions listed above?

_____

_____

_____

Appendix 3.3   Responsive Resources

Scan the QR codes to access the following resources as you continue to learn about how to eliminate microaggressions.

RESOURCE TYPE	TITLE	URL
Article	"4 Ways Teachers Can Address Microaggressions in the Classroom" by Kimberly Griffin *(Noodle)*	
Book	*Microaggression Theory: Influence and Implications* edited by Gina C. Torino, David P. Rivera, Christina M. Dapodilupo, Kevin L. Nadal, and Derald Wing Sue *(Wiley)*	
Podcast	"The Microaggressions of Mispronouncing a Student's Name" by Franchesca Warren, author *(The Educator's Room)*	
Video	"Microaggressions in the Classroom" *(Focused.Arts.Media.Education)*	

PART TWO

Focusing on Your Relationships

Co-Constructing Meaningful Connections With Students and Families

Vignette: Ms. Asia Henderson

Science Teacher, Grade 6

I am a sixth-grade science teacher at a charter middle school located in a major metropolitan area. This is my 8th year teaching. Earlier in my career, I taught at another charter middle school in the same city and served as a founding dean at a charter high school in another major metropolitan area. I also coach youth sports. My experiences as a teacher, coach, and school leader inform the ways that I connect with my scholars and their families.

When I began teaching at my current school, it was important for me to introduce myself to the parents the first week I arrived. I arrived at the school mid-academic year, and thankfully, the school leadership did not throw me right into the fire to start teaching right away. They assigned me an advisory, so I could begin building relationships with the scholars while observing classes throughout the week. This arrangement gave me time to start building relationships with parents.

The pandemic forced many educators to adjust the way that we teach our kids and the way our kids learn. During the height of the pandemic, my school moved to online teaching. However, as the COVID-19 case numbers decreased, the school adopted a hybrid model. For sixth grade, I taught three remote cohorts and two in-person cohorts. Our school leadership developed a schedule that catered to both online and in-person classes Monday–Thursday with all students, and teachers working remotely on Fridays. Teaching in person gives me the opportunity to be more up-close and personal with our kids. I get to see their body language and hear them out almost immediately when they have concerns. Aside from this, everything else stays the same.

I am very enthusiastic, energetic, and unapologetically authentic. My scholars know they can have fun with me, yet know to not cross the line and respect the space. I find myself being able to connect with scholars because I stay "hip" to what is current in the life of middle school children. This includes music, specific sayings that are "in season" and I tend to dress pretty cool for a teacher!

It is very important for my scholars to know who I am, where I come from, and how I carry myself. I am transparent about my sexuality, my family, and my teaching. By being intentional in expressing my pride in who I am, my scholars then know that they are safe and encouraged to be themselves. I am 100 percent authentic with molding our scholars to become well-rounded young children. It has always been important for me to model what it means to fully be yourself for my scholars to know that I support their lifestyle and constant self-adjustments in a positive way. They can see mistakes I make, and they can see me owning them. They have seen me put kids in their place, they have also seen me or experienced me pulling them aside to talk to them privately about life and personal things that only a teacher who has positive relationships with their scholars can do.

My school community has been really supportive and very big on embracing the cultural identity of not only its teachers and staff, but most important, the scholars. We conduct community meetings that address identity, and we teach scholars about what that can mean for others who identify as something else. Sometimes, my scholars say things that are not okay, and it has to do with their lack of knowledge, experience, and understanding. I usually use these instances as teachable moments. I'll call them out on it, and we have open discussions. Regardless, if I am teaching in person, online, or hybrid, I would talk to them just the same.

CHAPTER FOUR

Activating Students' Assets and Cultural Capital

REFLECTION QUESTIONS

Before delving into the chapter's contents, take a few minutes to work through the following reflection questions. There is space provided below for your responses. We revisit variations of these reflection questions at the end of the chapter.

- How do I leverage my students' assets to help them learn and succeed?

- In what ways have my students contributed to the overall learning environment?

- What do I see as my own limited understanding of seeing my students' strengths versus their deficits?

- What do I hope to learn from this chapter?

_____

_____

_____

_____

_____

_____

_____

THE VALUE IN HONORING ASSETS

Whether intentional or not, how we were raised and the images and messages we have received throughout our lives from loved ones, educators, and the media impact the way in which we carry out our teaching responsibilities. To be true culturally responsive educators, we need to acknowledge these things. We also need to work toward teaching from a new pedagogical perspective that identifies students' strengths and leverages those strengths to support their overall success.

The classroom does not mean just a physical space. Even within a virtual learning environment, culturally responsive teaching practices must remain; they may be even more critical in digital classrooms. Students in an online learning environment need ways to feel and stay connected with their teachers, classmates, and course content. When we honor what students bring to the class and value those contributions, even in different spaces, students feel like valued members of the learning community, which translates into higher levels of student engagement and success.

This chapter provides the content and practice you need to value and honor the assets of all your students in Dynamic Equitable Learning Environments (DELE) by:

- Discussing how a constructivist perspective can help reframe our mindsets toward growth

- Examining teacher expectations as related to looking at students' assets versus perceived deficits

- Discovering what cultural capital is and how valuing it in students can be useful in online learning environments

- Introducing Yosso's (2005) Community Cultural Wealth model as an assets-based teaching tool to leverage in DELE

- Exploring strengths-based approaches to teaching including asset mapping and verbal validation of students' contributions to the class community

As you read and engage in the different activities, think about your current, past, or future students. Think about some of the challenges you have faced with focusing on students' strengths, and use this time as an opportunity to develop a plan to ameliorate some of those concerns.

REFRAMING OUR MINDSET TOWARD GROWTH

Our past experiences may lead us to focus more on what needs to be fixed as opposed to developing what is there. We may even be coming to this work from a place of "my job as a teacher is to look at shortcomings of students and to fix them." And while supporting students is a critical part of an educators' role, the way in which we think about growth is equally crucial. It was only in the last decade that the Response to Intervention (RTI) model started to be used in place of the Discrepancy model, in identifying students for special education services. In short, the Discrepancy model waits for students to *fail* by not meeting a specific score on an IQ test. In contrast, the RTI model is a proactive approach and conducts universal assessments and supports to provide all learners with *tiers* of services, depending on their individual needs. In an assets-based classroom, from day one teachers get to know our students and their abilities and focus on helping them strengthen what is there and develop new competencies.

We can rely on educational theory to guide our work as we reframe our mindset toward growth. Looking at the works of both cognitive and social constructivists can provide supported lenses in developing culturally responsive teaching practices (Wachira & Mburu, 2019). Guiding culturally responsive teaching through the lens of constructivism can help shape our thinking as teachers to serve, support, and sustain our practices with all children, focused on growth (Algava, 2016).

Using a constructivist approach to teaching and learning includes experiential learning, collaboration, and inquiry, which will enable students to:

- Participate in **experiential learning** activities where they learn through practice and active engagement

- Work **collaboratively** with other students in the class, while getting to know their interests, beliefs, and perspectives

- Engage in learning activities focused on **inquiry** where students can discover and learn about new topics, cultures, and ideas

TEACHER EXPECTATIONS: A FOCUS ON ASSETS, NOT DEFICITS

Teacher expectations are linked to students' academic outcomes (Johnston et al., 2019; Wang et al., 2018). When teachers recognize potential in students, students believe in themselves and are more likely to perform well. When teachers have high expectations for students, they are more likely to excel and succeed. Teacher expectations matter (Papageorge et al., 2020).

Given the relationship between teacher expectations and student outcomes, it is important for teachers to recognize and capitalize on students' assets (López, 2017). Student assets are their strengths—including their dispositions, knowledge, talents, and skills (Nieto & Bode, 2018). Students' assets also reside in their families, communities, and cultural heritage (Nieto & Bode, 2018).

Getting to know your students helps reveal student assets that may not be readily apparent in an academic setting. We cover this more in Chapter 5. Assets-based teaching focuses on students' strengths and leverages those strengths to facilitate student learning. Developing an asset-based approach to teaching requires an intentional shift away from deficit mindsets. When we focus on problems instead of potential, we can limit our expectations of student learning and success. Moreover, it can influence how we approach teaching and the range of possibilities we see for problem solving. Usually, deficit-based mindsets see problems in student behavior and learning as inherent flaws, thereby limiting the approach to resolutions and dampening expectations for student success. With an asset-based approach to teaching, teachers do not see *problems*; they see *opportunities* for student learning.

Let's apply this asset-based shift to a virtual setting.

- The student who cannot sit still at the computer does not lack self-control based on their upbringing (deficit thinking), but instead might be bored with the text-based content on the screen because their attention activates in a more stimulating environment (asset thinking).

- The student who has difficulty typing long passages (deficit thinking) is actually a great blogger because they can express their thoughts quickly (asset thinking).

- The student who is struggling to learn English as a new language (deficit thinking) has digital fluency (asset thinking).

Instead of focusing on students' problems that need to be fixed, teachers can instead tap into students' talents and knowledge and build on their assets.

See Table 4.1 below for illustrations of what an asset-based approach looks like during live lessons, team projects, and one-on-one meetings. Examples of actionable behaviors that reflect an asset-based approach in virtual learning environments are provided.

Table 4.1 • Assets-Based Approaches in In-Person and Online Classrooms

	ASSET-BASED APPROACH	DELE EXAMPLES
During the lesson	Feedback focused on strengths such as, "Maya, such an insightful observation. That's a great interpretation of the story!"	**In Person:** Display positive, real-time, nonverbal cues throughout the lesson for formative assessment, for example, smiling and nodding to affirm a student's participation. **Online:** Utilize backchannel communication through chat boxes to provide real-time, nonverbal cues for students using emojis and icons.
Small team projects	Encourage students to work together to create solutions. Assign each team member an area of the project based on what you know their strengths are.	**In Person:** Provide students with a collaborative space to meet and work together on a shared goal. **Online:** Students meet in breakout rooms or use collaborative software. In-person students can have a technology device to access a virtual space where they will meet with students who are learning online, simultaneously.
One-on-one meeting	Affirm students' strengths and provide clear, direct constructive feedback on areas for growth.	**In Person:** Review student assignments together to acknowledge and commend strengths/areas of demonstrated growth, while highlighting areas for development and offering support to attain high expectations. **Online:** Have a progress chart on the screen during the virtual meeting so students can *see* how far they have come and inspire them on what is to come.

WHAT IS CULTURAL CAPITAL?

As we think about teacher expectations, it is important to consider the role of cultural capital in influencing what teachers see as assets and as deficits. Introduced with the French scholar Pierre Bourdieu, cultural capital is based on one's familiarity with the dominant culture within a society; it is the accumulation of knowledge, behaviors, and skills that are passed on through families and acquired in formal educational settings. Schools "primarily reflect the knowledge and values of the economically and culturally dominant groups in society, they validate and reinforce the cultural capital that students from those dominant groups already bring from home" (Nieto & Bode, 2020, p. 218). In other words, teacher expectations are largely calibrated to the standard of White, middle-class culture. As a result, we often judge students' forms and expressions of culture and knowledge in comparison to this norm.

Bourdieu (1986) explained that there are three forms of cultural capital:

1. **The Embodied State**: Dispositions of the body and mind, such as style of speech and dress

2. **The Objectified State**: Cultural goods such as art, books, and other material objects

3. **The Institutionalized State**: Academic qualifications and educational credentials

Current research has recently added a fourth form of cultural capital, *technical capital*, which is knowledge and skills with technology such as computers and the internet (Paino & Renzulli, 2012). This form of cultural capital has become increasingly important in an era when children are attending school remotely. Paino and Renzulli (2012) highlight the digital dimensions of cultural capital and suggest that computer proficiency should be "understood as a form of cultural capital within the context of the classroom" (p. 136). Their research suggests that "visible computer proficiency rather than mere access to computers is the key component to both direct and indirect benefits for students" (p. 136). It is not until the teacher sees and acknowledges a student's computer proficiency that the student can reap the rewards of the associated cultural capital.

As an educator, how can you adapt and develop asset-based practices that recognize and build upon the cultural capital that your students bring to the virtual classroom? Yosso's (2005) model of Community Cultural Wealth may offer direction.

THE COMMUNITY CULTURAL WEALTH MODEL: AN ASSETS-BASED TEACHING TOOL

The Community Cultural Wealth Model (Yosso, 2005) is an assets-based theory that can serve as a framework for educators to understand how, collectively, students are rich in cultural capital. The Community Cultural Wealth Model provides a strengths-based approach for teachers, who can leverage the assets that culturally and linguistically diverse students and their communities bring into educational settings. Because some of the different types of cultural capital may not be recognized in schools (Manzo et al., 2018), we need to be cognizant of the Community Cultural Wealth Model and make concerted efforts in tapping into each of the six forms of cultural capital identified by Yosso (2005) including: (1) aspirational, (2) linguistic, (3) familial, (4) social, (5) navigational, and (6) resistance.

Figure 4.1 • A Model of Community Cultural Wealth

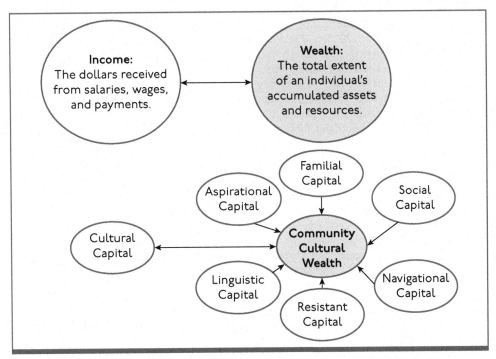

Source: Yosso, T. J. (2005). Whose culture has capital? *Race, Ethnicity and Education, 8I*(1), 69–91, 78. Used with permission.

Table 4.2 • Description and Examples of the Community Cultural Wealth Model

TYPE OF CULTURAL CAPITAL	DESCRIPTION	EXAMPLE
Aspirational	Highlights the positive perspective that families have for their children's education, regardless of the current realities of inequity in education (Yosso, 2005). This type of capital gives families "the ability to maintain hopes and dreams for the future even in the face of barriers" (Manzo et al., 2018, p. 342).	*Myra's family has discussed the importance of college from birth. It has always been "when" instead of "if" you go to college. Her room has been decorated with "swag" from the different colleges she is interested in. She has visited the campuses of local colleges. And, her family always connects what she is learning in her K–12 studies, to her future college studies.*

(Continued)

(Continued)

TYPE OF CULTURAL CAPITAL	DESCRIPTION	EXAMPLE
Familial	"[E]ngages a commitment to community well-being and expands the concept of family to include a more broad understanding of kinship" (Yosso, 2005, p. 79). Students come to school rich in human resources, experiences, and learning from family and community that can be leveraged in schools, if schools acknowledge this form of cultural capital.	*Lionnel has always been encouraged to seek out resources of extended family members and the larger community for support. When he needed support with an algebra assignment, his father recommended a chess coach who volunteered at the local community center.*
Linguistic	Focuses on the use of storytelling as a communicative vehicle and "includes the intellectual and social skills attained through communication experiences in more than one language and/or style" (Yosso, 2005, p. 79). According to Yosso (2005), with linguistic capital, students of color come to school with more than one way to communicate and use language. Often, schools do not recognize the different linguistic capital that students have if it is not consistent with the language and communicative devices used by the dominant group.	*Sammy can easily code switch and decipher languages, dialects, and meanings of words across various contexts. Because of this, Sammy can communicate with peers, adults, and others from different cultures.*
Social	Surrounds the more informal connections that students and families have that can assist them with upward mobility (Yosso, 2005). For example, attending and graduating college or securing a competitive internship by way of being connected with different professionals in their field of study. Through interactions in settings outside of school, students learn and connect with others, which creates social capital (Moloi, 2015). The more influence and power those students are socially connected with can greatly impact the school experience, and even what school the student attends or what teacher they have.	*Tanya is offered a competitive apprenticeship, without officially applying, through an associate of her dad who is a member of the same golfing club and owns a finance corporation.*

TYPE OF CULTURAL CAPITAL	DESCRIPTION	EXAMPLE
Navigational	Involves students' and their families' abilities to operate within structured institutions that may be hostile toward them (Yosso, 2005). More specifically, "navigational capital refers to skills of maneuvering through social institutions. Historically, this infers the ability to maneuver through institutions not created with Communities of Color in mind" (Yosso, 2005, p. 80). Educational institutions typically fit within this type of structure, where the content, curriculum, and operations are created with the dominant culture in mind.	*Martin's family knows that the curriculum at his college preparatory high school is based on the dominant culture, so they send him to 4 years of weekend and summer programming to prepare for success.*
Resistance	Is connected to social justice and the aspects within it that families have embedded in their children to influence change. Yosso (2005) states that "maintaining and passing on the multiple dimensions of community cultural wealth is also part of the knowledge base of resistant capital" (p. 80). Even in environments where they are not welcomed, students who are rich in resistance capital work together to find the resources to secure their rights and fight against injustices.	*Angel's mother reminds them every day that they will have to work harder than their peers who do not look like them, while encouraging them to maintain their willpower and fight to break through the barriers that they will face in school.*

By valuing students through the lens of their community cultural wealth, we can identify aspects of students' lived experiences and potential contributions that can be leveraged in ways not traditionally considered. As teachers, we may be challenged with identifying the different forms of cultural capital students bring and how the forms of cultural capital may be challenged in different online and in-person learning environments. Table 4.3 looks at each form of cultural capital, identifies how the form of cultural capital could be challenged in the online and in-person learning environments, and provides strategies for educators to leverage and sustain each form of cultural capital in K–12 DELE. The examples provided can be used for students being taught both online and in person.

Table 4.3 ◆ Leveraging and Sustaining Students' Cultural Capital Across Learning Environments

FORM OF CULTURAL CAPITAL	WHAT IT LOOKS LIKE FOR STUDENTS	HOW THIS CULTURAL CAPITAL IS CHALLENGED IN ONLINE AND IN-PERSON LEARNING ENVIRONMENTS	EXAMPLE IN K–12 DELE
Aspirational	Maintaining hopes and dreams despite barriers	Technology access and internet issues, which result in students not being able to access synchronous and asynchronous lessons.	• Meet with students via telephone when they cannot get online. For larger classes, map out a monthly calendar and call one to two students each day during the month. • Conduct regular check-ins to cover any missed materials. This can be done through small groups in-person or in virtual breakout rooms. • Advocate for students and their families at the school and district level and help them locate information on accessing reliable internet and getting devices to use for learning. • Ensure that students know that they have support, even from a distance, and constantly encourage them. • Take students on virtual campus visits and expose them to different college types.
Familial	Resources provided by family and social networks	Students may be home alone during the school day while their families are working. Or families may be working from home but not able to be fully present.	• Schedule virtual or phone conferences with families to get to know them, their schedule, background, and ways that they can contribute to their child's learning. • Create a classroom social media page or blog where classwork can be posted and updates provided. Or create a Pinterest board or Padlet where families can contribute materials to support student learning and share resources at times convenient for them.
Linguistic	Intellectual and social skills attained through communication experiences in more than one language or style	Students will need to "code switch" using a different dialect at home than they would at school, more frequently when they are online learning at home.	• Discover if students speak a different dialect or language at home and find out who in your school or district can provide support in translating materials for families. • Encourage students to use their home languages. Provide students access to online artificial intelligence tools such as Google Translate. • Use technology applications such as ClassDojo that can translate written communication into families' home languages.

FORM OF CULTURAL CAPITAL	WHAT IT LOOKS LIKE FOR STUDENTS	HOW THIS CULTURAL CAPITAL IS CHALLENGED IN ONLINE AND IN-PERSON LEARNING ENVIRONMENTS	EXAMPLE IN K–12 DELE
			• Allow pauses and be patient with students when responding to questions during the lesson. • Allow students to record responses in lieu of requiring live, on-the-spot answers.
Social	Informal connections that students and families have that can assist them with upward mobility	Students may not have anyone in their social networks who has experience with online teaching and learning, and the format may be a challenge for them and their families.	• Provide resources, tutorials, and screencasts for using every part of the online ecosystem (navigating learning modules, submitting assignments, participating, and communicating with peers and teachers). Scan the QR code to check out Kathy Schrock's Guide to Everything webpage for lots of ideas, tools *and* tips on screencasting in the classroom.
Navigational	Abilities and skills needed to navigate social institutions such as schools	Students may not be recommended and supported to take college preparation courses because of fear that the online environment will be too difficult for them. Also, students may be placed in low-level learning breakout groups during synchronous learning activities	• Develop a plan to help students successfully navigate the online platform in ways that leverage their strengths. • Allow students to choose which groups they are in. • Build breakout groups based on diverse ability levels of students where students can help one another learn.
Resistance	The courage and desire to fight against systemic injustices	Minoritized students and/or students at low income schools may be given all asynchronous learning and self-teaching through packets, while their peers at predominantly White and/or high income schools are offered hands-on and inquiry-based learning opportunities.	• Maintain high expectations for all students, regardless of the learning environment. • Find ways to provide student-centered and synchronous learning experiences for all students.

Some suggestions and starting points were listed in Table 4.3. Can you find others? Use the table below and share three examples of how three of the six types of your students' cultural capital could be leveraged or sustained.

ANTI-BIAS EXERCISE 4.1

TYPE OF CULTURAL CAPITAL TO LEVERAGE AND SUSTAIN *(i.e., aspirational, familial, linguistic, navigational, resistance, social)*	WHAT CAN YOU DO AS A TEACHER TO HELP LEVERAGE AND SUSTAIN THE FORM OF CULTURAL CAPITAL IN THE ONLINE LEARNING ENVIRONMENT?
1.	
2.	
3.	

STOP WORRYING ABOUT WHAT STUDENTS CAN'T DO! RELY ON STRENGTH-BASED APPROACHES INSTEAD

Particularly in the online environment, we necessarily bring attention to inequitable access issues that are coupled with previously existing educational gaps. However, focusing on what students cannot do is taxing, unmotivating, and certainly not responsive to the needs of all students. In this chapter, we have covered what students' cultural capital is, provided a framework from Yosso (2005) that explains the different types of capital that students have, highlighted the potential ways those capitals could be challenged in an online environment, and listed ways that teachers can build from those types of cultural capital in an online classroom.

Now, we look at strengths-based approaches to teaching culturally diverse students and what that looks like specifically in an online learning environment. Using strengths-based approaches can have a positive impact on students' success in schools (Galloway et al., 2020).

Asset Mapping

Asset mapping is a way that teachers can understand the lived experiences of students, the gifts that they bring to the classroom, and the larger context that influences students' overall development (Borrero & Yeh, 2016). Asset mapping allows us as educators to focus on what our community of learners bring, instead of spending time on deficits (Williment & Jones-Grant, 2011). After getting to know your students and their backgrounds, create a classroom community asset map. It will be helpful to revisit this after moving along to Chapter 5 on creating caring connections with all students and Chapter 6 on forging meaningful relationships with families and communities. Once you have drafted a copy of your asset map in this action planner, you can create it digitally as an infographic or mindmap. Once created, post a copy of the class asset map somewhere in your physical classroom or virtual classroom space within the learning management system you use. This will provide students with a daily reminder about the assets they bring to the class community.

ANTI-BIAS EXERCISE 4.2

MY CLASS ASSET MAP

Use the space below to map out the assets that your students bring to the classroom. There is no specific template for your class asset map, and every map will look different because they all have diverse students, whose experiences and backgrounds are unique. Consider using the following questions to support you as you develop your class asset map.

(Continued)

(Continued)

- Who are my students? What connections do my students have?

- What communities do they come from? What assets exist within their communities?

- What are some of the unique talents and strengths that my students hold?

- What contributions have my students made to the class thus far?

If you choose to create a digital class asset map, some tools that might be helpful include Canva, Visme, Emaze, or Adobe Spark.

We would love to see how you have developed your class asset maps. Please share and tweet us your class asset maps using the hashtag **#CRTinDELE (Culturally Responsive Teaching in Dynamic Equitable Learning Environments)** and tag @DrBudhai.

Verbal Validation and Affirmation

There is an old saying that "sticks and stones may break my bones, but words will never hurt me." And while that saying does some justice in helping students learn to ignore what is said about them, the reality is, words matter and can be especially hurtful and harmful. It can be argued that in virtual teaching and learning spaces, in particular, words matter even more. Through words, information and perspectives are communicated. When done via typed letters, it can be difficult to confirm the tone and manner in which words are being presented.

What and how we communicate our thoughts to students must be done in very intentional and respectful ways. Being a culturally responsive educator includes validating and affirming students' lived experiences, cultural backgrounds, and perspectives that they bring to the class community (De La Garza et al., 2020), and this must be communicated verbally to students. When we are communicating with students, we can provide them with verbal validation and affirmation by:

- **Acknowledging** the strengths students bring in particular academic disciplines

- **Valuing** students' thoughts, perspectives, and beliefs and ensuring that they hear you

- **Empowering** students to use their knowledge to continue to grow and develop, helping build their self-esteem and self-efficacy

- **Co-Creating** learning experiences with students, asking them to work with you and share their knowledge

- **Celebrating** small and large wins, telling students how proud you are of what they have accomplished and what is to come

ANTI-BIAS EXERCISE 4.3

We've just talked about how to verbally validate and affirm students. Let's practice! Revise the following statements in a way that is focused on strengths and would make students feel validated.

Example: Tori, your desk area looks very cluttered and is distracting during live lessons.

Revised: <u>Tori, I noticed you have unique items on your desk during our live lessons; it would be great if you would share some of the things during our Friday share time. Our class community would benefit from getting to know what items are special to you.</u>

Thelonious, I see you answered three of the ten math questions incorrectly.

_____

_____

Tina, your 90-degree angle looks more like a 100-degree angle.

_____

_____

Kandy, helping Mike spell a word does not require you to play your Nintendo Switch in the background.

_____

_____

WHAT'S NEXT?

Now that we have explored asset-based teaching approaches, we move to Chapter 5, which is focused on integrating the intersections of students' identities. Remember to put all the content and newly learned information from this chapter into action. Use the provided action plan template to tease out how you will focus on your students' assets and leverage their cultural capital. You can also check your understanding first by completing the culturally sustaining checklist below.

REFLECTION QUESTIONS

You have worked through Chapter 4 and explored the importance of focusing on students' assets, as opposed to their deficits, and learned various strengths-based approaches that can be leveraged within the online teaching and learning environment. Take a few minutes to read through and reflect on the following questions. They may seem familiar because they are variations of the ones you completed prior to reading this chapter. Once you have recorded your responses, go back to the beginning of the chapter to see how your knowledge, awareness, and skills surrounding activating students' assets and cultural capital have expanded.

- How will I leverage my students' assets to help them learn and succeed?

- In what ways have my students contributed to the overall learning environment?

- What will I continue to work on to strengthen my understanding of seeing students' strengths?

- What are the key takeaways that I will take from this chapter into my practice?

_____

_____

_____

_____

_____

_____

Appendix 4.1

Culturally Sustaining Checklist: Toward an Assets-Based Mindset

On a scale of 1–4, please select how much you agree or disagree with the following statements.

| 1 = Strongly Disagree | 2 = Disagree | 3 = Agree | 4 = Strongly Agree |

ON A SCALE OF 1–4, INDICATE YOUR LEVEL OF AWARENESS.	AWARENESS	NOTES FOR FURTHER DEVELOPMENT:
	I am aware of my implicit biases related to student assets and potential.	
	I am aware of what deficit thinking is.	
	I am aware of the impact that deficit thinking can have on student growth.	
ON A SCALE OF 1–4, INDICATE YOUR LEVEL OF KNOWLEDGE.	KNOWLEDGE	NOTES FOR FURTHER DEVELOPMENT:
	I know the difference between looking at students' assets and deficits.	
	I understand the assumptions informing my expectations of students.	
	I know that my approach to teaching will impact all students feeling valued.	
ON A SCALE OF 1–4, INDICATE YOUR LEVEL OF SKILL.	SKILLS	NOTES FOR FURTHER DEVELOPMENT:
	I can articulate the importance of activating students' assets.	
	I can approach teaching from a strengths-based mindset.	
	I can create a map of the assets that my students bring to the classroom community.	

Appendix 4.2

Action Plan: How Will I Work Toward Activating my
Students' Assets and Cultural Capital?

What are three actions you can take to use what you have learned in this chapter to activate your own students' assets and cultural capital?

1.

2.

3.

What supports or information do you need to successfully complete the three actions you listed above?

1.

2.

3.

What challenges and barriers do you expect to be faced with in carrying out the three actions you listed above, and what ideas do you have for addressing them?

CHALLENGES/BARRIERS	IDEAS TO ADDRESS THEM
1.	
2.	
3.	

How do you expect your students to benefit from you taking the three actions listed above?

_____

_____

_____

Appendix 4.3 Responsive Resources

Scan the QR codes to access the resources listed below so you explore to continue to learn about valuing your students' assets.

RESOURCE TYPE	DESCRIPTION	URL
Article	"Shifting the Paradigm from Deficit Oriented Schools to Asset Based Models: Why Leaders Need to Promote an Asset Orientation in our Schools" by Shannon Renkly and Katherine Bertolini *(Empowering Research for Educators)*	
Book	*Strengths-Based Teaching and Learning in Mathematics: Five Teaching Turnarounds for Grades K–6* by Beth McCord Kobett and Karen S. Karp (Corwin)	
Podcast	"Asset Based Pedagogy With Dr. Francesca López" (Leading Equity Podcast)	
Video	"Overcoming Deficit-Oriented Approaches to Teaching" (The Art of Making Meaning)	

CHAPTER FIVE

Caring for Students Within Their Sociopolitical Contexts

REFLECTION QUESTIONS

Before delving into the chapter's contents, take a few minutes to work through the following reflection questions. There is space provided below for your responses. We revisit variations of these reflection questions at the end of the chapter.

- What is the harm in the statement: "I don't see color; I treat all my students the same"?

- Why is it important to know and understand your students' cultural identities within the current sociopolitical context?

- Why is it important to incorporate students' identities into the curriculum?

- How do I form caring and culturally responsive relationships with my students?

- What do I hope to learn from this chapter?

_____

_____

_____

_____

_____

THE IMPORTANCE OF CARING STUDENT-TEACHER RELATIONSHIPS

Our first job as teachers is to make sure that we learn our students, that we connect with them on a real level, showing respect for their culture and affirming their worthiness to receive the best education possible.

—James Ford, 2015 North Carolina State Teacher of the Year

Research shows caring teacher-student relationships are associated with the following short-term and long-term measures of student performance and outcomes, including:

- Attendance

- Grades

- Fewer disruptive behaviors and suspensions

- Lower school dropout rates (Sparks, 2019)

Related studies also show that teachers benefit from caring relationships with their students. Teachers report higher student academic engagement and greater joy teaching (Sparks, 2019).

This chapter provides the content and practice you need to develop caring relationships with culturally and linguistically diverse students in Dynamic Equitable Learning Environments (DELE) by:

- Defining care and colorblindness

- Situating students in their larger sociopolitical context

- Understanding the teacher's role in students' webs of care and support

- Understanding identity and intersectionality

- Developing strategies to establish and build caring relationships with students

As a result of completing these different activities, you will learn what it means to care for minoritized and marginalized students in ways they can see, understand, and feel. We invite you to reflect on your past and current relationships with students. Use the space of this chapter to understand your role at the nexus of cultural identity and learning.

UNDERSTANDING YOUR ROLE IN CHILD AND YOUTH DEVELOPMENT

Bronfenbenner's Bioecological Systems Theory includes teachers and schools as central figures in the lifeworlds of children and youth. He details five systems to explore and explain the different forces and influences in child development. Each of these systems is nested, with bidirectional relationships within and among the five systems below:

- **Microsystem:** the people and institutions with whom the focal person has daily or near-daily contact (family, school, place of worship, community)

- **Mesosystem:** the relationships between people in the microsystem AND how these relationships influence the development of the focal person (parental relationship, parents-siblings, parents-school, parents-community, school-community, parents-place of worship, school-place of worship, etc.)

- **Exosystem:** people and institutions with whom the focal person has no relationship, but who make decisions that directly impact the focal person (parents' employers, school board, city government, police department, owner of the local grocery store, university president, and board of trustees, etc.)

- **Macrosystem:** societal, national, and international decisions and events (the media), state/federal legislation (for example, education, foreign policy, the economy, the media, etc.), and international events (wars, natural disasters, Olympics, etc.)

- **Chronosystem:** personal background and historical events; consider how the sociopolitical context would be different if a student was born 50 years earlier or later, and imagine the difference in educational and social access/opportunities available to them.

Figure 5.1 below provides a graphic depiction of the relationship between these five systems.

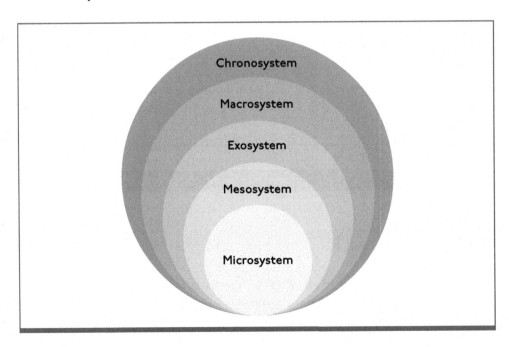

Alongside their parents and families, teachers and schools are invaluable members of a student's life. You are part of the web of care and support necessary for healthy child growth and development. There are few relationships as central and significant as that of the teacher-student relationship. You are entrusted with the care of each of the students in your classroom.

ANTI-BIAS EXERCISE 5.1

Identify and describe three aspects of your students' sociopolitical context that shape their lived experiences and life chances.

1.

2.

3.

DEFINING CARE

Noted philosopher Noddings's (2003) framework for an ethic of care has informed scholars and teachers alike. She emphasizes reciprocity as an essential element of care in relationships between teachers and students.

Teachers expressing their care for students is insufficient. Students must both recognize and receive the care being offered by teachers. Noddings (2003) explains that "no matter how hard teachers try to care, if the caring is not received by students, the claim 'they don't care' has some validity. It suggests strongly that something is very wrong" (p. 15). Without reciprocity, a caring relationship cannot exist.

Despite the power of Noddings' conceptualization of care, her definition is incomplete when we consider the experiences of students of color and other marginalized student populations. Rolòn-Dow (2005) generated a new theory, a critical care praxis. She explains that "to care for students of color in the United States, we must seek to understand the role that race/ethnicity has played in shaping and defining the sociocultural and political conditions of their communities" (p. 103). She insists that teachers need to first demonstrate their care by understanding how issues of racism, sexism, classism, heterosexism, and other forms of oppression have affected the communities and schools where their students live and learn.

ANTI-BIAS EXERCISE 5.2

After reading Noddings's and Rolòn-Dow's theories of care, define what care means to you.

_____

_____

_____

_____

THE INCOMPATIBILITY OF CARE AND COLORBLINDNESS

Let's begin this section with an anti-bias exercise.

ANTI-BIAS EXERCISE 5.3

Instructions: Indicate your level of agreement with each of the statements below.	STRONGLY DISAGREE	DISAGREE	AGREE	STRONGLY AGREE
"I don't see color. I only see students."				
"I don't see Black or White. I treat all my students the same."				
"I don't care what LGBTQ students do. I just don't want to see it in my classroom."				
"I treat all my students fairly and equally."				
"I don't think of my students in terms of what makes them different. I am color-blind when it comes to my teaching."				

Colorblindness is "the idea that ignoring or overlooking racial and ethnic differences promotes racial harmony" (Scruggs, 2009, para. 5). Many teachers profess to be color-blind in their interactions with students of color. Teachers can also profess to wear *blinders* for other kinds of human differences, such as gender and sexual orientation. Statements such as those listed above in Anti-Bias Exercise 5.3 suggest that to be color-blind is to be fair and objective.

Unfortunately, the opposite is true. Nieto and Bode (2018) suggest that "colorblindness may result in *refusing to accept differences* and therefore accepting the dominant culture as the norm" (p. 136). Being blind to student differences denies the identities and experiences of particular groups of students. Such denials can render students invisible and contribute to teachers underestimating the true potential of minoritized and marginalized students.

Seeing your students is a necessary step to caring for and about them. You cannot be color-blind and care for all your students; the two are incompatible. It is important to recognize student differences and see the beauty, talent, and potential in all students.

SEEING ALL STUDENTS: IDENTITY AND INTERSECTIONALITY

As mentioned in the Introduction, the student population in the United States is becoming increasingly diverse. American classrooms reflect the rich diversity of the world. As culturally responsive educators, we recognize the wonderful array of cultures, languages, abilities, and histories that our students possess. Each of our students has a complex identity "shaped by individual characteristics, family dynamics, historical factors, and social and political contexts" (Tatum, 2003, p. 18). Students have multiple identities including race, ethnicity, gender, socioeconomic status, sexual orientation, ability, religion and/or spirituality, and others.

Intersectionality is defined as "the social, economic, and political ways in which identity-based systems of oppression and privilege connect, overlap, and influence one another" (Bell, 2016, para. 5). Intersectionality should inform how we see our students. It is important that we do not reduce students to one aspect of their identities, but that we learn about and appreciate the constellation of identities that make our students who they are. Moreover, the intersections of students' complex identities shape their experiences in schools (Crenshaw, 1989). As culturally responsive educators, we should work to identify and disrupt the school policies and practices that subject our students, particularly girls of color and LGBT students of color, to unique forms of disadvantage and discrimination (Crenshaw, 1989).

As culturally responsive educators, we need to be sensitive to how our students' intersectional identities shape their experiences in school. For example, African American girls are more likely to be disciplined, suspended, and expelled from school than other girls (Morris, 2016). Generally mistaken for being older than they are, African American girls often receive punishments that are disproportionate to the perceived infractions. The raced and gendered experiences of African American girls compound the kinds of discrimination they experience in schools.

GETTING TO KNOW YOUR STUDENTS

The first step in getting to know your students is to learn to pronounce their names. Pronouncing your students' names is part of your first interaction. Kohli and Solorzano (2016) explain some of the ways that

Scan this QR code to watch the video "Getting Students' Names Right: Why It Matters" from *Education Week*.

mispronouncing students' names can impact them. Our names are symbolic of our family, culture, and heritage. When we correctly pronounce students' names, they feel respected and included. When students' names are mispronounced, they feel disrespected and alienated. Worse, some teachers attempt to laugh off their error mispronouncing a student's name by mocking the student's name or making it seem that the student is the problem for having a *difficult* name. Worse still, some teachers assign students nicknames, changing their names and forgoing the effort to learn the names of the students in their classrooms. These are examples of racial microaggressions and, for too many students, teachers mispronouncing their names is a consistent part of their schooling experiences (Kohli & Solorzano, 2012). To learn more about why pronouncing students' names matter, scan the QR code. Also, see Table 5.1 for additional strategies to correctly pronounce your students' names.

Table 5.1 • Strategies to Correctly Pronounce Your Students' Names

Use Index Cards
This is an oldie but goodie. Write down students' names with the correct phonetic pronunciation. You can also use the app *Pronounce Names*; however, the accuracy is not 100 percent guaranteed.
Play a "Name Game"
In either in-person or online classes, ask students to pronounce their name and share the story behind their names (i.e., why they were given their name). When students finish, thank them for sharing and say their name with the correct pronunciation. For students in online classes, this activity can be recorded; this enables you to replay and practice pronouncing each student's name.
NameCoach
Name Coach provides audio recordings of people saying their names, making it much easier to both learn and remember how to say a name.

Ask students what they wish to be called. This is particularly important for transgender and gender-nonconforming students. Similar to mispronouncing a student's name, refusing to use a student's preferred name and pronouns has the effect of disrespecting, ostracizing, and rendering a student invisible. There are no legal constraints preventing teachers and school staff from referring to transgender and gender nonconforming students by their preferred names and pronouns (Kosciw et al., 2015).

After learning your students' names, it is important to remember their names. In online classrooms, remembering students' names can be relatively easy because most apps list the individual's name at the bottom of their onscreen image. However, when you meet students in person, you will not have the benefit of the app. Table 5.2 shares strategies to remember students' names.

Table 5.2 • Strategies to Remember Your Students' Names

Take Pictures
Take pictures of your students, and write their names under their images. Or take pictures of students while they are wearing name badges/signs. Review the pictures before class.
Name Tents
Provide students with blank name tents, and invite them to decorate them on the first day of class. Have markers, stickers, and other arts and crafts items on hand!
Practice Saying Your Students' Names
Greet students by name when they enter the classroom. Not only will this help you remember students' names, but it will also create a sense of belonging and community in your class. This also works with online classes!

Learning and remembering students' names are the first steps. Table 5.3 lists four ways to get to know students in in-person and online learning environments.

Table 5.3 • Four Ways to Get to Know Students in In-Person and Online Learning Environments

	IN-PERSON	**ONLINE**
Surveys	Pass out a hard copy of a survey, and ask students to complete and return it. The survey can include items that ask about students' favorite things, past travels, likes, and dislikes. You choose the focus of the survey.	Using Survey Monkey, Google Forms, or a similar tool, create a survey to learn about your students. (Electronic surveys can be used with in-person students, too.)
Individual meetings	Schedule individual meetings with students at the beginning of the academic year to learn about them, their families, their interests, and their learning styles. These individual meetings can take place in person and online. Following this formal meeting, you can also connect informally with students before, during, or after class.	In virtual settings, this might include communicating with students via the chat feature in Zoom or asking students to stay after class to continue a discussion. Office hours are another wonderful way to meet with students individually, both in person and online.
Autobiographical assignments	Invite students to complete assignments that entail student discussion of their identities, backgrounds, and aspirations. These assignments can be written accounts, photo documentaries, video recordings, or mixed media. A student's creativity can say as much about them as the assignment that they produce. Technological tools can be used in both in-person and online settings.	

(Continued)

(Continued)

	IN-PERSON	ONLINE
Show and tell	Invite students to bring an artifact that represents who they are, or represents an important event in their lives, for show and tell. In person, the assignment will need to be assigned in advance so that students can identify and bring an item to school with their parents' permission.	Online students can be told in advance. However, if this is a same-day activity, students should be given sufficient time to locate an artifact that they feel comfortable sharing with the class.

WHAT'S NEXT?

In this chapter, we explored caring culturally responsive relationships between teachers and students. First, we unpack colorblindness and explain why a color-blind approach to relationships with students does not result in care. Then we take a deeper dive into care as part of a culturally responsive approach to teacher-student relationships. We define care and the conditions necessary to express care in ways that minoritized and marginalized students can recognize and receive it. We conclude the chapter with a look at strategies to establish caring relationships across Dynamic Equitable Learning Environments.

Earlier in Chapter 5, we discussed how teachers are part of a dynamic web of support surrounding each student. In Chapter 6, we take a closer look at two important connections in this web: school-family relationships and school-community relationships. As culturally responsive educators, these relationships are vital to forming a strong web of care and support around our students.

REFLECTION QUESTIONS

You have worked through Chapter 5 and explored the importance of caring for students in their sociopolitical contexts. Take a few minutes to read through and reflect on the questions below. They may seem familiar because they are variations of the ones you completed prior to reading this chapter. Once you have recorded your responses, go back to the beginning of the chapter to see how your knowledge, awareness, and skills surrounding your understanding of the role of caring for students within in-person and online culturally responsive teaching have expanded.

- What does care mean to me?

- Why is it important to know my students' cultural identities within the current sociopolitical context?

- Why is it important to incorporate students' identities into the curriculum?

- How do I form caring, culturally responsive relationships with my students?

- What are the key takeaways that I will take from this chapter into my practice?

_____

_____

_____

_____

_____

_____

_____

_____

_____

_____

_____

_____

_____

_____

Appendix 5.1

Culturally Sustaining Checklist: Caring for
Students within their Sociopolitical Contexts

On a scale of 1–4, please select how much you agree or disagree with the following statements.

| 1 = Strongly Disagree | 2 = Disagree | 3 = Agree | 4 = Strongly Agree |

ON A SCALE OF 1–4, INDICATE YOUR LEVEL OF AWARENESS.	AWARENESS	NOTES FOR FURTHER DEVELOPMENT:
	I am aware of the benefits of caring teacher-student relationships.	
	I am aware of the incompatibility of colorblindness and culturally responsive teaching.	
	I am aware of the importance of having students' identities reflected in the classroom community.	
ON A SCALE OF 1–4, INDICATE YOUR LEVEL OF KNOWLEDGE.	KNOWLEDGE	NOTES FOR FURTHER DEVELOPMENT:
	I know that it is important to understand my students' identities within their sociopolitical context.	
	I know that it is affirming to correctly pronounce and remember my students' names.	
	I know that forming caring relationships with my students will help facilitate their learning.	
ON A SCALE OF 1–4, INDICATE YOUR LEVEL OF SKILL.	SKILLS	NOTES FOR FURTHER DEVELOPMENT:
	I can develop my cultural competence by educating myself about the histories of my students' various cultural groups and the current sociopolitical contexts.	
	I can use Bronfenbrenner's Bioecological Systems model to identify the other members in my students' webs of care.	
	I can employ different approaches to building caring relationships with my students.	

Appendix 5.2

Action Plan: How Will I Care for My Students in
Their Sociopolitical Contexts?

What are three actions you can take to care for students within their sociopolitical contexts?

1.

2.

3.

What supports or information do you need to successfully complete the three actions you listed above?

1.

2.

3.

What challenges and barriers do you expect to be faced with in carrying out the three actions you listed above, and what ideas do you have for addressing them?

CHALLENGES/BARRIERS	IDEAS TO ADDRESS THEM
1.	
2.	
3.	

How do you expect your students to benefit from you taking the three actions listed above?

_____

_____

_____

Appendix 5.3   Responsive Resources

Scan the QR codes to access the resources listed below as you continue to learn about culturally responsive approaches to caring for your students in person and online.

RESOURCE TYPE	TITLE	URL
Article	"Culturally Responsive Education as an Ethics- and Care-Based Approach to Urban Education" by Rae Shevalier and Barbara Ann McKenzie *(Urban Education)*	
Book	*Cultural Competence Now: 56 Exercises to Help Educators Understand and Challenge Bias, Racism, and Privilege* by Vernita Mayfield (ASCD)	
Podcast	"Creating Moments of Genuine Connection Online" (Cult of Pedagogy)	
Video	"Creating Caring and Culturally Responsive Classrooms for Students in Prekindergarten to Grade 3" (Institute of Education Sciences)	

CHAPTER SIX

Forging Reciprocal Relationships With Families and Communities

REFLECTION QUESTIONS

Before delving into the chapter's contents, take a few minutes to work through the following reflection questions. There is space provided below for your responses. We revisit variations of these reflection questions at the end of the chapter.

- What does reciprocity look like in the context of my relationships with my students' families and communities?

- How do I overcome barriers to communication with my students' families?

- How do I establish meaningful collaborations with the leaders and organizations in my students' communities?

- How do I learn about and leverage the funds of knowledge possessed by my students' families and communities?

- How do I forge meaningful partnerships with my students' families and communities to facilitate student learning?

_____

_____

_____

_____

THE IMPORTANCE OF FAMILY-SCHOOL-COMMUNITY RELATIONSHIPS

Consistently, research has shown that parent involvement in their children's education contributes to positive student outcomes (Henderson & Mapp, 2002). Students whose parents are involved in their education are:

- More likely to attend school

- Less likely to have behavior issues

- Less likely to be suspended or expelled from school

- More likely to perform well on academic assessments

- More likely to get promoted to the next grade

- More likely to graduate from high school

These results are true across race/ethnicity, gender, and socioeconomic status (Henderson & Mapp, 2002).

As educators committed to the success of all students, how can we partner with our students' families and communities to facilitate student learning and success? In this chapter, we examine and explore teachers' relationships with culturally and linguistically diverse families and communities. We draw on the principles and practices of culturally responsive pedagogy to inform the ways teachers establish and sustain relationships. This chapter provides the content and practice you need to forge partnerships with your students' families and communities in Dynamic Equitable Learning Environments (DELE) by:

- Understanding the importance of teachers, families, and communities forming networks of and in support of student learning and success

- Reimagining Epstein's six types of parent involvement in DELE

- Recognizing visible and invisible types of parent involvement in their children's education

- Discovering funds of knowledge in families and communities

- Developing culturally responsive strategies to overcome barriers to communication and build bridges to collaboration

As a result of completing this chapter, you will explore culturally responsive approaches to engage culturally and linguistically diverse families and communities. We encourage you to reflect on your strengths in

...

connecting with families and communities, as well as the areas where you can grow. Use the space of this chapter to consider ways you can forge authentic, reciprocal partnerships with your students' families and other caring adults in their microsystems.

UNDERSTANDING THE RELATIONSHIPS BETWEEN TEACHERS, PARENTS, AND COMMUNITY IN STUDENT LEARNING AND SUCCESS

As discussed in Chapter 5, Bronfenbrenner's Bioecological Systems Theory emphasizes the significance of relationships in child development. School, family, and community are each part of a child's microsystem. Each of these institutions—and, more important, the people within them—plays a critical role in the development of a child. While the microsystem reflects the child's individual relationships with each institution, the mesosystem is composed of the relationships between each of the institutions in the microsystem. The relationships between the primary people in a child's life have a powerful influence on a child's development.

Here in Chapter 6, we take a closer look at the mesosystem. The mesosystem is comprised of the relationships between people/institutions in the student's microsystem. See Figure 6.1 below for a depiction of the mesosystem formed by the family and school in relation to the child.

Figure 6.1 • Mesosystemic Depiction of How the Relationship Between Family and School Affects a Child

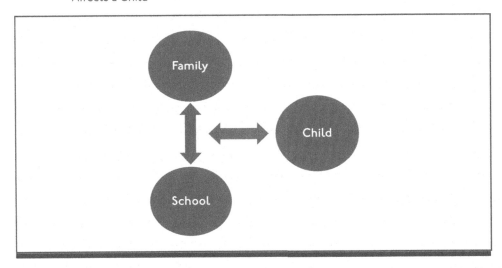

As core members of a child's microsystem, the relationship between the teacher and parent is influential. In other words, if the relationship between the teacher and parent is friendly and collaborative, the student is likely to benefit and feel supported. Conversely, if the relationship between the teacher and parent is argumentative and combative, the student is likely to be adversely affected and feel unsupported. As caring adults in the student's microsystem, it is important for teachers and parents to be on the same page where the student is concerned.

WAYS TO INVOLVE FAMILIES AND COMMUNITIES IN SCHOOLS

Generally, when we think of parent involvement in schools, we think of one of the six types of involvement codified by Joyce Epstein (2010), founder of the National Network of Partnership Schools at Johns Hopkins University. Schools recognize parent involvement as parents and families supporting children's learning. This can be accomplished by promoting learning at home by reading with children and frequenting educational sites such as visiting museums. Parents can also support their children's learning by ensuring their children are ready to learn at the start of each school day, attending report card conferences and other school events, and volunteering to help with school functions. Parents are key members of the school community, and their involvement can help ensure a vibrant dynamic equitable learning environment. Epstein's (2010) Framework of Six Types of Involvement is provided in Table 6.1.

Table 6.1 • Epstein's (2010) Framework of Six Types of Involvement (p. 85)

Type 1: Parenting	Help all families establish home environments to support children as students.
Type 2: Communicating	Design effective forms of school-to-home and home-to-school communications about school programs in children's progress.
Type 3: Volunteering	Recruit an organized parent to help and support.
Type 4: Learning at Home	Provide information and ideas to families about how to help students at home with homework and other curriculum-related activities, decisions, and planning.
Type 5: Decision Making	Include parents in school decisions, developing parent leaders and representatives.
Type 6: Collaborating With Community	Identify and integrate resources and services from the community to strengthen school programs, family practices, and student learning and development.

We are all familiar with what each of these types looks like in a brick-and-mortar school. For example, parenting (Type 1) may include workshops to teach parents strategies to assist their children with reading at home, or volunteering (Type 3) may include parents volunteering to help teachers chaperone a field trip. We may be less familiar with what these types look like in the virtual environment.

Table 6.2 • Examples of Epstein's Framework of Six Types of Involvement in Online Learning Environments

Type 1: Parenting	Hold a virtual workshop via Zoom to make suggestions to parents on how to create learning spaces in the home conducive to their children's learning.
Type 2: Communicating	Share weekly reports with parents on their children's progress via ClassDojo.
Type 3: Volunteering	Coordinate parent volunteers to serve as Parent Mentors to support families who are new to the online learning environment by assisting them with navigating the learning management system and other online portals and/or processes.
Type 4: Learning at Home	Provide parents with access to an online classroom handbook via Google Drive that includes the homework policy and schedule, as well as a calendar with important dates of classroom activities and school events.
Type 5: Decision Making	Create a classroom parent advisory board, and invite parents to attend meetings via Google Meet.
Type 6: Collaborating With Community	Teachers invite representatives from family-oriented organizations to be part of a virtual community fair where they describe services available to support children and families engaged in online learning.

These are just a few examples of ways that the six types of parent involvement can be translated into online learning environments. Can you imagine three more? Use the space below to brainstorm ways that you could involve families and communities in your online teaching and learning.

ANTI-BIAS EXERCISE 6.1

Stop and Reflect: Use the space below to brainstorm ways that you could involve families and communities in your online teaching and learning.

_____

_____

_____

_____

_____

_____

_____

_____

VISIBLE AND INVISIBLE WAYS THAT PARENTS ARE INVOLVED IN THEIR CHILDREN'S EDUCATION

The six types of involvement described above represent traditional practices that schools employ to involve parents in their children's education. Often teacher-initiated, these types of involvement require parents to be involved in their children's education on the school's terms. Communication is often one-way, from the teacher or school to the parents or families in formats such as flyers, emails, robocalls, or social media announcements that may not allow for response or dialogue. Teachers often see parents as _help labor_ to assist with tasks. For example, in the classroom and at home, parents can help teachers "reduce their own workload and [compensate] for resources" and leave teachers "empowered . . . to do their own job both effectively and efficiently" (Christianakis, 2011, pp. 9–10). In this traditional approach to parent involvement, parents are not seen as equal partners, and the relationships between the family and school are not built on trust and reciprocity (Henderson et al., 2007).

As culturally responsive educators, we know that these traditional types of parent involvement are based on White, middle-class norms. As such, the norms and related expectations of parents may be difficult for culturally and linguistically diverse families to attain. For immigrant families, expectations for family involvement may be unclear. Due to cultural differences, they may have a different conceptualization of their role as a parent in their children's education. For some parents, school may have been a site of trauma where they may have experienced bullying or violence. As a result of their own negative experiences in school, they do not attend events at the school. For other parents, they are unable to attend school happenings because of conflicts with their work schedules or other competing obligations. For a host of reasons, these traditional types of parent involvement are not inclusive of all parents. However, this should not be interpreted as evidence that parents do not care or the family is not involved.

Take a minute to complete Anti-Bias Exercise 6.2 and consider reasons why the actions of culturally and linguistically diverse families may be misunderstood.

ANTI-BIAS EXERCISE 6.2

Can you think of a time when you felt like a parent did not care about their child's education? What contributed to this? Can you identify two ways that the parent supported their child's education that might have been invisible to you?

_____

_____

_____

_____

_____

_____

_____

In contrast to White, middle-class norms associated with traditional types of parent involvement, culturally responsive approaches to family engagement recognize the assets, strengths, and cultural capital that culturally and linguistically diverse families possess. Parents are not seen as problems, but partners in their children's education. As such, parents are valued for their involvement in their children's education and their investment in the school community. Culturally responsive educators begin forging relationships with culturally and linguistically diverse families by establishing communication.

GETTING TO KNOW FAMILIES AND COMMUNITIES

As culturally responsive educators, engaging in the process of getting to know your students' families and communities entails learning about the funds of knowledge. Gonzalez et al. (2005) developed the Funds of Knowledge approach that encompasses learning about the daily lives, cultural tools, and knowledge of students and their families. By drawing on these funds of knowledge, "student experience is legitimated as valid, and classroom practice can build on familiar knowledge bases that student can manipulate to enhance learning" (Gonzalez et al., 2005, p. 43). Moreover, teachers can begin to establish trust with families by listening and learning about their lived experiences, cultural practices, knowledge, and skills. Examples of funds of knowledge can include learning how to make tamales from scratch or how to repair a car.

When you interview families to learn about their funds of knowledge, you have an opportunity:

1. To initiate relations of trust with families to enable discussion of their practices and funds of knowledge; and

2. To document these lived experiences and knowledge that may prove useful in defining households, individually and collectively, as having ample resources or assets that may be valuable for instruction. (Moll, 2019, p. 132)

Such knowledge of your students' families and households can be treated as cultural resources for teaching and learning (Moll, 2019). Funds of Knowledge will enable you "to identify and establish the educational capital of families often assumed to be lacking any such resources" (p. 132). Home visits can be a viable way to learn about families' funds of knowledge. See Table 6.3 for ideas on how to conduct these practices in person and online.

Table 6.3 • Home Visits: In Person and Online

	IN PERSON	**ONLINE**
Home Visits	Schedule the home visit at a time that is convenient for the family. Recognize the time and energy that the family may put into preparing for your visit, and consider bringing a gift such as doughnuts for a morning visit or cookies for an afternoon visit. Adopt a learning and listening stance. The visit should last approximately 30 minutes.	If possible, arrange to meet with the parent using a convenient and familiar technology. For some parents, this might be their cell phone using Duo, FaceTime, or Facebook Messenger. For others, this might involve a computer or tablet using a service such as Skype or Zoom. Adopt a learning and listening stance. The visit should last between 20 and 30 minutes.

PARTNERING WITH COMMUNITIES: IN PERSON AND ONLINE

As the third element of students' microsystems, the community is an integral part of children's development and learning. As culturally responsive educators, learning about the community is important to understanding your students and their families.

School–community partnerships are beneficial for several reasons. Students benefit from these partnerships through positive student outcomes, expanded networks, and increased knowledge of the community. Community partnerships also benefit teachers and schools as they can complement the school curriculum, and increase school resources in the form of mentors, advocates, and sponsors. Community partners also benefit from the relationship with the schools because they can support student learning in meaningful and *real-world* ways, inform students and families of their services, and access resources available through the school (i.e., space, staff, etc.).

ANTI-BIAS EXERCISE 6.3

Identify three assets and strengths in the local and virtual community available to your school.

I.

(Continued)

2.

3.

Identify two ways that you can leverage these assets and strengths to engage students in learning.

1.

2.

Identify two ways that you can leverage these assets and strengths to support families.

1.

2.

Now, we describe two approaches to learn about and partner with people in your students' community: community walks and service learning.

Scan this QR code to read the article "Community Walks Create Bonds of Understanding" from *Edutopia.*

Whether virtual or in person, community walks are one approach to learning about your students and their families. Community walks can be transformative. You follow in your students' footsteps, taking the same route, passing the same businesses and buildings that they walk by every day. Community walks will teach you about the neighborhood's assets and resources. You will see the places where your students and their families live—where they work, worship, shop, relax, and play. Community walks can dispel myths and stereotypes about neighborhoods and humanize the people who live there. When students are the guide, community walks can instill a sense of pride and convey care. Community walks are a way to build bridges between families, schools, and communities.

Please scan the two QR codes to find instructions for conducting a community walk. The first example includes guidance for conducting a general community walk led by students. The second example integrates math concepts.

Service-learning projects are also a wonderful way to forge partnerships with members of the community. Schools and communities benefit from service-learning projects because student learning is enhanced, and the community organization can raise awareness about its focal issue. The community agency can benefit from student involvement, as well as the opportunity to see neighborhood youth in a new light as engaged members of the community. Importantly, students benefit from the experience. Service learning can develop students' skills with communication, collaboration, and leadership. Students also can build relationships in their own communities. Scan the QR code for examples of service-learning projects.

Scan this QR code to view a community walk activity from TEACH Math.

Scan this QR code to view service-learning lesson plans from Roots and Shoots.

COMMUNICATING WITH CULTURALLY AND LINGUISTICALLY DIVERSE FAMILIES

Establishing relationships with your students' families begins with communication. To be reciprocal, the communication needs to be two-way. More than communicating with parents to inform them about their child or a school-related event, use communication channels to listen and learn about the child's family and life at home. Use technology to your advantage. Table 6.4 highlights three apps that can help facilitate teacher-parent communication, both in in-person and online settings.

Table 6.4 ◆ Three Communication Apps

	FEATURES
Google Voice Google Voice, attached to your personal mobile number, allows you to create an alternate phone number you might share with parents (to avoid using your personal cell phone number).	No need for multiple devices—all calls come to one cell number; option to answer or redirect to voicemail after answering the call; messages accessible via email; voice messages also translated to written emails; ability to text and call from a number other than your personal cell.

(Continued)

(Continued)

	FEATURES
<u>ClassDojo</u> ClassDojo is a classroom management app with which you can also communicate students' progress with their parents. 	Enables parents to visualize progress; provides Positive Behavioral Interventions and Supports for students; embedded features to support remote learning (such as student portfolio submissions).
<u>Remind</u> Remind is an opt-in app that sends messages to subscribers. Parents sign up once and get reminders via text to their cell phones. 	Can be used on a smartphone or a computer; can send and receive an unlimited number of messages.

Adapted from https://www.edutopia.org/article/using-technology-connect-parents

WHAT'S NEXT?

With the conclusion of Chapter 6, you have also completed Part II. You have explored how to employ culturally responsive practices to construct meaningful relationships with students, their families, and communities. Now, it is time to turn your attention to curriculum and instruction. In Part III, you will consider ways to develop culturally responsive pedagogies and practices into your teaching in in-person and online settings. In Chapter 7, you will begin with adopting an equity mindset and consider ways to foster an equitable classroom culture. In Chapters 8 and 9, you will learn about the integration of cultural content into the curriculum and assessment, respectively. As a culturally responsive educator, Part III offers a space for you to reflect and explore how you create the dynamic equitable learning environments for your relationships with students, families, and communities to flourish.

REFLECTION QUESTIONS

You have worked through Chapter 6 and explored the importance of forging reciprocal relationships with families and communities. Take a few minutes to read through and reflect on the questions below. They may seem familiar because they are variations of the ones you completed prior to reading this chapter. Once you have recorded your responses, go back to the beginning of the chapter to see how your knowledge, awareness, and skills surrounding your understanding of culturally responsive family and community engagement practices have expanded.

- How will I ensure reciprocity in my partnerships with my students' families?

- How will I employ technology and other available resources to communicate with my students' families?

- How will I incorporate the funds of knowledge available in my students' families and communities to engage student learning in my classrooms?

- How will I create and sustain constructive relationships with members of my students' communities?

- What are the key takeaways that I will take from this chapter into my practice?

_____

_____

_____

_____

_____

_____

_____

_____

_____

_____

Appendix 6.1

Culturally Sustaining Checklist: Forging Reciprocal
Relationships With Students' Families and Communities

On a scale of 1–4, please select how much you agree or disagree with the following statements.

| 1 = Strongly Disagree | 2 = Disagree | 3 = Agree | 4 = Strongly Agree |

ON A SCALE OF 1–4, INDICATE YOUR LEVEL OF AWARENESS.	AWARENESS	NOTES FOR FURTHER DEVELOPMENT:
	I am aware of some of my implicit biases related to culturally and linguistically diverse families.	
	I am aware of what reciprocity means in teacher-parent partnerships.	
	I am aware of the reasons why family, school, and community partnerships are important.	

ON A SCALE OF 1–4, INDICATE YOUR LEVEL OF KNOWLEDGE.	KNOWLEDGE	NOTES FOR FURTHER DEVELOPMENT:
	I understand the assumptions informing my expectations of parents and families.	
	I know Epstein's framework for six types of involvement with families and communities.	
	I know that the way I communicate with families will affect the trust and reciprocity I try to establish.	

ON A SCALE OF 1–4, INDICATE YOUR LEVEL OF SKILL.	SKILLS	NOTES FOR FURTHER DEVELOPMENT:
	I can articulate the importance of partnering with my students' families and communities.	
	I can conduct interviews with my students' families using the Funds of Knowledge framework.	
	I can partner with leaders and representatives of relevant community organizations for the benefit of my students and their families.	

Appendix 6.2

Action Plan: How Will I Work to Forge Reciprocal
Relationships With My Students' Families and Communities?

What are three actions you can take to use what you have learned in this chapter to forge reciprocal relationships with your students' families and communities?

1.

2.

3.

What supports or information do you need to successfully complete the three actions you listed above?

1.

2.

3.

What challenges and barriers do you expect to be faced with in carrying out the three actions you listed above, and what ideas do you have for addressing them?

CHALLENGES/BARRIERS	IDEAS TO ADDRESS THEM
1.	
2.	
3.	

How do you expect your students to benefit from you taking the three actions listed above?

_____

_____

_____

Appendix 6.3   Responsive Resources

Scan the QR codes to access the resources listed below to continue to learn about partnering with your students' families and communities.

RESOURCE TYPE	DESCRIPTION	URL
Article	"Why I'm not involved: Parental involvement from a parent's perspective" by Jung-Ah Choi *(Phi Delta Kappan)*	
Book	*Powerful Partnerships: A Teacher's Guide to Engaging Families for Student Success* by Karen L. Mapp, Ilene Carner, and Jessica Lander *(Scholastic)*	
Podcast	"Transforming Schools through Parent Engagement" (Classnotes Podcast—Intercultural Development Research Association)	
Video	"School–Community Partnerships for the Whole Child: Learning from Comprehensive Models Series—Webinar 3: Partner with Families" (New America)	

PART THREE

Focusing on Your Pedagogical Practices

Incorporating Culturally Relevant Teaching

Vignette: Mr. Khemar Journey

Mathematics Teacher, Grades 9–12

I am a high school mathematics teacher in a major urban school district. I am approaching the beginning of my 7th year in the classroom. Earlier in my career, I taught at a magnet school. In my current school, I teach students in general, honors, and AP math classes, ranging from algebra I and II through calculus and statistics. I also teach math courses at a community college and a major local university. Like most teachers across the country, I had not taught online prior to the pandemic.

Regardless of whether I'm teaching in person or online, I try to get to know all my students and make every student feel that they are important. I felt like I needed to do more to get to know my students in the online environment, especially those who were unable or unwilling to turn on their cameras. I felt like I had to know them because I had to give them a reason to come to class. So I tried to get to know them all, and I learned about their backgrounds and experiences. I also shared my background with them so that they can understand that our backgrounds and experiences are similar. As a result, I can tailor some of my teaching to their experiences and interests. Building relationships with students is really so very important.

The first few minutes of every class, I notice what's happening in the room and I'll talk about it. Maybe I notice what someone is doing, or maybe it's their background, or even a picture in the background. I'll ask about it, and we end up in a conversation. We talk about their stories—what's going on, what's happening in school, what's happening in life, what's happening in the culture. I find that because there's always conversation, students will want to come to class. I have experienced that when class is dismissed, and the last period is over, students do not want to leave!

I don't see myself just as a math teacher. I see where my students are, and I teach them to question and interrogate the world. In my racially diverse school, the racial stratification is striking in my classes. My honors classes have predominantly White students, and my general math classes have predominantly Black and Brown students. I know that the school system has discarded many of the Black and Latinx students in my general mathematics courses. The school's expectations for them are low. They will not have the opportunity to take AP courses, and they are not expected to go to college. I don't go into those classes thinking, "I need to just teach you math." I go into those classes thinking, "I need to also teach you life, that this is what people expect of you; this is what this path looks like; let's figure out how we can change it."

CHAPTER SEVEN

Developing Equity-Minded Practices

REFLECTION QUESTIONS

Before delving into the chapter's contents, take a few minutes to work through the following reflection questions. There is space provided below for your responses. We revisit variations of these reflection questions at the end of the chapter.

- How do I describe equity-minded practices?

- What does it mean to decolonize learning environments?

- How do I build an anti-racist online and in-person classroom culture?

- What do I hope to learn from this chapter?

_____

_____

_____

_____

_____

_____

_____

SHIFTING MINDSETS

Welcome to Part III of this action planner! In this chapter, we shift our focus to mindsets. More specifically, developing equity mindedness. First, we should discuss what a mindset is. According to the *Merriam-Webster Dictionary* (2021), mindset can be described as "a mental attitude or inclination" or "a fixed state of mind" (para. 1). Let's break these definitions down some as it relates to teaching and learning. An attitude is the way you feel or your emotion toward something. In the classroom, your attitude can lead you toward not supporting high-stakes testing, for example. An inclination is your disposition. You may be more inclined to conference with a guardian about a student's challenging behaviors instead of automatically sending the student to detention. Simply put, attitudes and inclination shape how we approach situations, our thinking around issues, and how we go about our work as an educator.

While attitude and inclination seem to be more fluid, the second definition of mindset, which is having a state of mind that is fixed, does not. This is why it is important that we shift our mindsets, wherever they may be, toward equity. And if they are already there, then great, we can go even deeper toward social justice. As culturally responsive educators, we have to be open, flexible, and willing to change our perspectives, based on new knowledge. Think back to Part I in this book, and the work you did to not only acknowledge the implicit and explicit biases that you may bring into the class, but also your development of an action plan for eliminating microaggressions that may have been previously intentionally or unintentionally directed toward students; we do something similar in this chapter on developing equity mindedness.

In this chapter, we provide you with strategies and tools that can be leveraged as you shift your attitudes, inclinations, and mindsets toward Dynamic Equitable Learning Environments (DELE) by:

- Discussing the ways in which teachers can shift their mindsets

- Exploring the impact of colonization on classrooms along with strategies to decolonize online and in-person learning environments

- Describing the ways teachers can build an anti-racist online and in-person class culture

- Reviewing the impact that equity-minded and anti-racist teaching practices can have in shaping DELE

We hope that as you read through this chapter's content on developing equity mindedness, you think closely and critically about your current and past mindsets including attitudes, inclinations, and states of mind, and how they have impacted the way in which you interact with and teach students. This chapter includes a host of strategies, ideas, and anti-bias exercises that we hope will encourage you and guide your shifting mindset.

ENACTING EQUITY-MINDED PRACTICES

The University of Southern California's Rossier School of Education's Center for Urban Education (2021) explains that "equity-minded practitioners are aware of the racial and ethnic inequities ingrained in our society and intentionally work to address them" (para. 7). It is not enough to understand one's own bias or even appreciate the tenets of a multicultural education curriculum, although it is a starting place and why we begin this action planner doing just that. To teach with equity in mind, we must acknowledge the systemic racism that has perpetuated school systems and contributed to the achievement gap between White students and culturally and linguistically diverse students. We realize that "developing equity mindedness requires time and experiences beyond what the undergraduate TEP [teacher education program] can provide" (Lazar, 2018, p. 316) and are hoping to use this chapter to help you start to develop equity-minded practices. Think about some of the structures that currently exist within your classrooms, your school, and your school district that may have contributed to the disparities in teaching and learning that your students face.

ANTI-BIAS EXERCISE 7.1

A MINI PRE-EQUITY AUDIT

As mentioned above, to be equity-minded we must look holistically at how social inequities impact our students. Respond to the following questions to the best of your ability, based on the information you currently have, by circling one of the bolded options in each statement below:

I)   Compared to other school districts in the state, my school district has access to **insufficient, adequate,** or an **abundance** of funding to provide the needed resources for all students in the district.

(Continued)

(Continued)

2) All students in the school have **strong**, **moderate**, or **poor** internet bandwidth required to access online curriculum materials.

3) When it comes to student discipline, my school uses a **restorative justice** or **punitive** system.

4) The curriculum that my school or school district requires us to use is **embedded with** or **does not include** the tenets of multicultural education, showing the perspectives and examples of content from different perspectives, people, and cultures.

5) The online library repository includes a **low**, **medium**, or **high** volume of books that are reflective of the lived experiences of the diverse student body.

We hope that going through the mini pre-equity audit exercise (Anti-Bias Exercise 7.1) ignited your thinking around the difference between equity and equality. Think about it in this way: If there was an opportunity to give away clothes to students, it would not be enough to give any student any item of clothing. We would ensure that all students not only have enough clothes to wear, but also have the clothing they need and the clothing that fits them.

Equity is not about making sure that every student has the same thing; it's about making sure that every student has what they each need. Equity is about making sure each student has the exact clothing they need, in the size that fits them. Equality, on the other hand, is about making sure every student has the same thing: equal access, equal opportunity, equal education. Equality and equity are both important, but they are different things. Table 7.1 shows some examples of equality vs. equity within in-person and online learning environments.

As culturally responsive teachers, we must ensure that the decision making, structures, and policies are equitable and just and meet the individual needs of each and every student regardless of whether they are learning online or in person.

Table 7.1 • Equality vs. Equity Within Online and In-Person Learning Environments

	EQUALITY		EQUITY	
	ONLINE	**IN-PERSON**	**ONLINE**	**IN-PERSON**
Funding	Every school receives $15,000 per year, per student	Every school receives $15,000 per year, per student	Every school receives an amount of funding that is reflective of the specific needs of the number of students who will learn online. More funding may be geared toward technology infrastructure and teacher training to instruct in online environments.	Every school receives an amount of funding that is reflective of the specific needs of the number of students who will learn in person. More funding may be geared toward food services and physical building maintenance.
Curriculum materials	Each student receives the same curriculum materials and supplies.	Each student receives the same curriculum materials and supplies.	Students are provided with access to the curriculum materials in an electronic format.	Students are provided with physical curriculum materials.
Technology	Each school receives one computer per student. All teachers have access to the same technology applications.	Each school receives one computer per student. All teachers have access to the same technology applications.	Each student receives a laptop with an internet router hotspot with high bandwidth capabilities.	Each student has access to a laptop or tablet device. The school building has high-speed Wi-Fi internet access.

DECOLONIZING ONLINE AND IN-PERSON LEARNING ENVIRONMENTS

Almost every society has dealt with the colonization of people, land, and other goods, in some capacity. Regardless of whether the most recent iteration of colonization occurred years ago, the impact is still very present. In learning environments, in particular, structures, policies, and practices have been built through the constructs of colonization. Only recently with increased visibility of civil unrest and protest in the country of racial injustices have issues surrounding the impact and effects on colonization been highlighted more widely. You may be thinking that these issues are bigger than you, and that makes sense because some of these issues do go beyond the purview of our classrooms. Rest assured, you will be provided with additional strategies to use your power for sustainable and equitable action in the Epilogue of this book. However, we do want you to be cognizant of the reality that aspects of colonization occur at the classroom level in both online and in-person learning environments. Remember:

> Textbooks and core curriculum are manifestations of the culture of power. It is imperative that we take a closer look at these texts that we have been assigned and for some, passively assigning to our young people. We cannot contribute to the erasure of history. It is our responsibility as educators to take steps in finding texts that not only showcase the voices and stories of our students and their ancestors but prioritize and humanize them beyond a month on the calendar. (PBS, 2020, para. 7)

Scan this QR code to read the article "*Lies My Teacher Told Me, and How American History Can Be Used as a Weapon.*"

In Chapter 8, we look more closely at planning an anti-bias curriculum, so it is important to understand the role that colonization has played in the disparities and discrepancies in schools. To be culturally responsive teachers, we must work toward decolonizing online and in-person learning environments. Best-selling author and the Oliver Cromwell Cox Award for Distinguished Anti-Racist Scholarship awardee James W. Loewen's book, *Lies My Teacher Told Me*, is a critical example of how textbooks in schools can perpetuate colonization. The first step is not only recognizing this, but also calling them out and providing alternatives where all sides of historical events, lived experiences, and multiple perspectives are being honored.

We have included a QR code to an *NPR* article that summarizes an interview with *Lies My Teacher Told Me* book author James W. Loewen.

ANTI-BIAS EXERCISE 7.2

Stop and Reflect: Now that you have focused your attention on how teaching and learning have been compromised by colonization, in addition to the curriculum, in what other areas have you seen this? Jot down your responses in the space provided below.

BUILDING ANTI-RACIST ONLINE AND IN-PERSON CLASSROOM CULTURES: CULTIVATING BRAVE SPACES

Building an anti-racist classroom culture begins with establishing ground rules for how students will communicate and interact with one another in the classroom setting. Generally, we think of creating safe spaces as a necessity for conversations about race. In their book chapter, "From Safe Spaces to Brave Spaces," Arao and Clemens (2013) outline the challenges with safe spaces and the promises of brave spaces. They (2013) explain that safe space is a "terminology we hope will be reassuring to participants who feel anxious about sharing their thoughts and feelings regarding these sensitive and controversial issues" (p. 135). When facilitating conversations about race and other identity and social justice topics, culturally responsive educators "have a responsibility to foster a learning environment that supports participants in the challenging work of authentic engagement" (Arao & Clemens, 2013, p. 139). Before we go further, let's get your thoughts on safe spaces.

ANTI-BIAS EXERCISE 7.3

When I think about facilitating conversations about race with my students,

I feel _____

_____

_____

I feel confident that I can _____

_____

_____

I would like to develop my skills in the areas of

_____

_____

_____

Safe spaces need to be interrogated. For whom are these spaces safe? Are these spaces *safe* for all students, and to equal degrees? Arao and Clemens (2013) argue that safe spaces are not safe for White students or students of color. They contend that "authentic learning about social justice often requires the very qualities of risk, difficulty, and controversy that are defined as incompatible with safety" (p. 139). Participating in conversations about race and social justice can be very difficult for White students. Confronted with evidence of their own unearned privilege and challenges to their unexamined worldviews often results in one of two responses: guilt and hopelessness and/or resistance and denial (Arao & Clemens, 2013). In neither instance do White students feel *safe* in the spaces of these discussions.

Neither do students of color feel safe in *safe spaces*. Given the history of oppression and injustice in the United States, as well as their own personal experiences, students of color know "that to name their oppression, and the perpetrators thereof, is a profoundly unsafe activity" (Arao & Clemens, 2013, p. 141). Students of color are aware that if they genuinely share their experiences and emotions, their interpretations of their own lived experiences might be questioned or invalidated, or they may be "dismissed and condemned as hypersensitive or unduly aggressive" (Arao & Clemens, 2013, p. 141). Students of color are also aware of the burden of White guilt (Sensoy & DiAngelo, 2014) and the expectations that they be understanding and engage in ongoing dialogue with their White peers. Arao and Clemens (2013) explain that the experiences of students of color, too, "are inconsistent with the definition of safety" (p. 141).

Recently, culturally responsive educators have endeavored to co-construct brave spaces with their students. Borrowing from Boostrom's (1998) critique of the idea of safe space, Arao and Clemens (2013) concur that "bravery is needed in these conversations because 'learning necessarily involves not merely risk, but the pain of giving up a former condition in favour of a new way of seeing things'" (p. 141; p. 399 in the original text). Such conversations require bravery and courage (Singleton, 2014) to engage in honest critical self-reflection, to share with one's teacher and peers, and to listen to the experiences of one's peers. Arao and Clemens (2013) share that from their own experiences, simply using the term "brave space" at the beginning of a class discussion can transform "a conversation that can otherwise be treated merely as setting tone and parameters . . . into an integral and important component of the [learning experience]" (p. 142).

Let's take a minute to consider what safe spaces and brave spaces look like in in-person and online learning contexts.

Table 7.2 ♦ Comparing Safe Spaces and Brave Spaces in In-Person and Online Learning Environments

	IN-PERSON LEARNING ENVIRONMENTS	ONLINE LEARNING ENVIRONMENTS
Safe spaces	The discussion of the class' ground rules is taken for granted. Students' suggestions for the ground rules are accepted and not interrogated. White students and students of color may experience varying levels and degrees of *safety* and discomfort during conversations about race and other social justice issues.	The discussion of the class' ground rules is largely taken for granted but does take into consideration the ways that technology can help or hinder the discussion (asynchronous vs. synchronous). Students' suggestions for the ground rules are accepted and not interrogated. White students and students of color may experience varying levels and degrees of *safety* and discomfort during conversations about race and other social justice issues.
Brave spaces	The discussion of the class' ground rules is not taken for granted. Students' suggestions for the ground rules are interrogated for how they may differentially and disproportionately affect certain students based on their identities and positionality. White students and students of color expect to experience discomfort and take risks in conversations about race and other social justice issues.	The discussion of the class' ground rules is not taken for granted, and the ways that technology can shape equitable participation in the discussion are considered. Students' suggestions for the ground rules are interrogated for how they may differentially and disproportionately affect certain students based on their identities, positionality, and access. White students and students of color expect to experience discomfort and take risks in conversations about race and other social justice issues.

Once the ground rules are established for your in-person and/or online learning environment, you can turn your attention to the facilitation of class discussions and student learning. Sensoy and DiAngelo (2014) recommend that educators with social justice commitments should guide students in:

1. Critical analysis of the presentation of mainstream knowledge as neutral, universal, and objective;

2. Critical self-reflection of their own socialization into structured relations of oppression and privilege; and

3. Developing the skills with which to see, analyze, and challenge relations of oppression and privilege. (pp. 2–3)

For further guidance on facilitating discussions about race and social justice topics with students, check out this guide and webinar presented by Learning for Justice (formerly Teaching Tolerance).

Learning for Justice (formerly Teaching Tolerance)

Let's Talk: Facilitating Critical Conversations With Students [Guide]

This guide offers classroom-ready strategies you can use to plan discussions and to facilitate these conversations with your students.

Let's Talk: Discussing Race, Racism, and Other Difficult Topics With Students [Webinar]

This webinar serves as a foundation to help build your capacity to safely broach these issues, and you'll walk away with use-tomorrow strategies.

Additional on-demand webinars are available on the Learning for Justice website including topics on bullying and bias, class, gender and sexual identity, immigration, race and ethnicity, religion, rights and activism, and slavery.

Next, we consider how class ground rules govern student discussions and interactions in DELE.

ANTI-BIAS EXERCISE 7.4

Now that you have devised your approach to co-constructing ground rules for the classroom culture with your students, how will you facilitate student learning and discussions with them? In the space below, identify three potential barriers to an equitable classroom community along with three possible ways you can overcome them.

Three potential barriers to an equitable classroom community

1.

2.

3.

Three possible ways that you can overcome these barriers

1.

2.

3.

There are important challenges and opportunities associated with facilitating courageous conversations about race and other social justice topics in online classroom settings. For asynchronous classrooms, the conversations may take place through written contributions to the discussion boards or video recordings posted via VoiceThread or Flipgrid. The challenge with each of these scenarios is that students cannot engage in such discussions in real time. Tone can still be interpreted in asynchronous responses, which leaves room for misunderstandings. There is an absence of body language and other nonverbal cues that are critical to effective communication. However, there are also advantages to asynchronous online discussions. Asynchronous discussions can be more equitable and democratic. Shy and introverted students who often find it difficult to participate in in-person classroom discussions can freely express themselves in a written discussion board, or read prepared remarks in a video recording. The asynchronous nature of the discussion allows more time for students to listen, reflect, and craft their responses.

For synchronous online classes, the challenges and advantages to the discussion are a blend of both in-person and asynchronous discussions. Regarding the challenges, students may have varying degrees of presence in the class. Student participation may be affected by the quality of their internet access. For varying reasons, students may turn off their cameras, or their cameras may be on but they are doing something distracting to the conversation at hand (such as playing with a pet or looking down at their phone). While the video may give some sense of students' body language, it provides an incomplete picture. The advantages of synchronous online discussions are that students can engage in real-time discussions. You can take advantage of different technologies and strategies to help facilitate the discussion. For example, the breakout group tool in Zoom enables online instructors to approximate small group discussions that would happen in an in-person setting.

Being equity-minded in the collaborative construction of class ground rules with your students will enable you to co-create DELE.

WHAT'S NEXT?

In his book, *How to Be an Antiracist*, Ibram X. Kendi (2019) teaches us, "The opposite of racist isn't 'not racist.' It is 'anti-racist.' . . . One either allows racial inequities to persevere, as a racist, or confronts racial inequities, as an anti-racist. There is no in-between safe space of 'not racist'" (p. 9). In Chapters 8 and 9, you will deepen your understanding of the relationship between culturally responsive teaching and anti-racist education. In Chapter 8, you will explore anti-racist approaches to curriculum development and, in Chapter 9, you will consider anti-racist approaches to assessment. Collectively, the chapters in Part III will extend your understanding of culturally responsive pedagogies and practices.

REFLECTION QUESTIONS

You have worked through Chapter 7 and explored ways to develop equity-minded practices within in-person and online learning environments. Take a few minutes to read through and reflect on the reflection questions below. They may seem familiar because they are variations of the ones you completed prior to reading this chapter. Once you have recorded your responses, go back to the beginning of the chapter to see how your knowledge, awareness, and skills surrounding equity-minded practices have expanded.

- How do I describe equity-minded practices?

- What does it mean to decolonize learning environments?

- How do I build an anti-racist online and in-person classroom culture?

- What have I learned from this chapter?

_____

_____

_____

_____

Appendix 7.1

Culturally Sustaining Checklist: Developing Equity-Minded Practices

On a scale of 1–4, please select how much you agree or disagree with the following statements.

| 1 = Strongly Disagree | 2 = Disagree | 3 = Agree | 4 = Strongly Agree |

ON A SCALE OF 1–4, INDICATE YOUR LEVEL OF AWARENESS.	AWARENESS	NOTES FOR FURTHER DEVELOPMENT:
	I am aware of what equity-minded practices are.	
	I am aware of the different ways to cultivate my own equity mindedness.	
	I am aware of how my own equity mindedness can affect learning for my students.	
ON A SCALE OF 1–4, INDICATE YOUR LEVEL OF KNOWLEDGE.	**KNOWLEDGE**	**NOTES FOR FURTHER DEVELOPMENT:**
	I know the definition of equity mindedness.	
	I know the difference between safe spaces and brave spaces for conversations about race and other social justice topics.	
	I know the value of equity-minded practices in my own teaching and learning.	
ON A SCALE OF 1–4, INDICATE YOUR LEVEL OF SKILL.	**SKILLS**	**NOTES FOR FURTHER DEVELOPMENT:**
	I can enact my equity mindedness when I co-create brave spaces in DELE with my students.	
	I can carry out equity-minded practices when I facilitate discussions in DELE with my students.	
	I can refine my own equity mindedness and its role in how I enact teaching and learning with my students.	

Appendix 7.2

Action Plan: What Actions Will I Take to Develop Equity-Minded Practices?

What are three actions you can take to use what you have learned in this chapter to assist you with developing equity-minded practices, decolonizing online and in-person learning environments, and employing anti-racist teaching practices?

1.

2.

3.

What supports or information do you need to successfully complete the three actions you listed above?

1.

2.

3.

What challenges and barriers do you expect to be faced with in carrying out the three actions you listed above, and what ideas do you have for addressing them?

CHALLENGES/BARRIERS	IDEAS TO ADDRESS THEM
1.	
2.	
3.	

How do you expect your students to benefit from you taking the three actions listed above?

_____

_____

_____

Appendix 7.3   Responsive Resources

Scan the QR codes to access the following resources as you continue to learn about developing equity-minded practices.

RESOURCE TYPE	TITLE	URL
Article	"Respect differences?: Challenging the Common Guidelines in Social Justice Education" by Ozlem Sensoy and Robin DiAngelo *(Democracy & Education)*	
Book	*How to Be an Antiracist* by Ibram X. Kendi (Penguin Random House)	
Podcast	"More than Just a Buzz Word-Embedding 'Equity Mindedness' for Concrete Change" (edWebcasts)	
Video	"Nihi! KIDS TALK about Decolonization" (Nihi! Kids)	

CHAPTER EIGHT

Planning Anti-Bias Instruction

REFLECTION QUESTIONS

Before delving into the chapter's contents, take a few minutes to work through the following reflection questions. There is space provided below for your responses. We revisit variations of these reflection questions at the end of the chapter.

- To my understanding, what is anti-bias instruction?

- How do I include the lived experiences and cultures of all students in the class, beyond heroes and holidays?

- Why is it important to include multiple viewpoints when teaching?

- What do I hope to learn from this chapter?

_____

_____

_____

_____

_____

_____

_____

_____

INSTRUCTION THAT *IS* FREE FROM BIAS

This chapter focuses on planning and implementing anti-bias instruction in online and in-person classrooms. Anti-bias instruction grew out of early childhood education using Derman-Sparks and ABC Task Force's (1989) *Anti-bias Curriculum Tools for Empowering Young Children*, which was published by the National Association for the Education of Young Children. And although much of the published work on anti-bias education is focused on young children, the basis and structure of it has relevance for all ages and can be translated into PK–12 settings. You might be thinking, "How exactly do I keep instruction free from bias," because in Chapter 1 we discussed unconscious bias and how we may bring perceptions, views, and stereotypes to the classroom that we are unaware of. Similar to the anti-bias exercises you completed in Part 1, you have to bring those reflections and acknowledgments into your work as you develop curriculum and content for students and the way in which you go about instructing them.

In Chapter 7, you learned about what anti-racist teaching is and how it can impact online and in-person learning environments. In this chapter, we build on this and discuss pedagogical strategies you can leverage as you develop culturally responsive curriculum and lessons for students in your Dynamic Equitable Learning Environments (DELE). To incorporate the lived experiences of all students and demonstrate to them that you value them, their families, and communities, the way we develop and teach them must be grounded in anti-bias instruction. Remember:

> In an effort to engender a climate of respect, educators often employ measures aimed at reducing bias and increasing mutual understanding of differences. While well intentioned, many of these strategies (e.g., organizing an assembly or a day of action) tend to be misguided, short-term solutions and occur at the individual level, thereby limiting the potential for sustainable change. (Gonzalez & Kokozos, 2019, p. 345)

In this chapter, we provide you with content and pedagogy needed to create, plan, and implement sustainable anti-bias instruction within your DELE by:

- Discussing the importance of going beyond heroes and holidays and when exposing students to different cultures within the curriculum

- Highlighting the ways that an anti-racist curriculum can be embedded into teaching and learning

- Describing how to honor multiple viewpoints and perspectives when teaching in online and in-person learning settings

- Reviewing culturally responsive content that can be leveraged within different content areas

While reading through this chapter's content, we hope that you continuously think about your own culturally responsive teaching practices and how they can be enhanced to go beyond the traditional ways of including diversity into curriculum and instruction.

MOVING BEYOND HEROES AND HOLIDAYS

Celebrating diversity is a small act that is often the one and only action teachers take to show that they are trying to be culturally responsive. First, there is the school calendar, which is generally out of our control as teachers. Each year, selected holidays are observed and many of them are connected to specific religions or cultures. Some schools look at the total student body of the school district and base their school holidays on when they believe a critical mass of students may be off of school due to their religion and/or cultural beliefs. Looking at the student body makeup to see what days more students would likely not attend school due to a religious or cultural holiday may serve the school. However, this does not necessarily teach students about why they are off of school, and there is usually no connection to the curriculum. Then there are holiday celebrations in school that typically occur in December, where only a couple of mainstream holidays are recognized.

Culturally responsive teaching goes well beyond a one-off cultural or diversity day where different cultures are highlighted with foods and clothing. Similarly, we must move beyond celebrating and acknowledging historical figures once a year, such as Dr. Martin Luther King Jr. Day, or Rosa Parks during February, because their experiences are not representative of every Black student in our classes (Wright, 2019). This is not to say that we should not acknowledge the contributions that different Black Americans and diverse groups have made to the country and world. What we are saying is that we should do this every day, for all races and ethnicities that are reflected in our student body through the curriculum.

ANTI-BIAS EXERCISE 8.1

Think about the ways you have *celebrated* diversity in your class or school, and respond to the following questions.

I have celebrated the diversity of my students by _____

_____

(Continued)

(Continued)

I acknowledge the religious and cultural holidays of my students by _____

_____

I can build on what I am currently doing to go beyond heroes and holidays by _____

_____

Instead of treating a small minority of persons of color and women as these greater-than-life heroic figures that are representative of all people who look like them, embed teaching about events, people, and religious customs within the context of the curriculum. Do not shy away from teaching about the tough topics such as slavery, the Holocaust, the Civil Rights Movement, and the colonization of America along with the resulting genocide of Indigenous Americans. Table 8.1 provides just a sprinkling of how to connect the contributions, lived experiences, and cultures of diverse people and groups into different academic subjects. This by all means is not an exhaustive list but can get you started.

Table 8.1 • Connecting Cultures to the Curriculum

Art	Teach students about the contributions of artists from around the world: • **Augusta Savage** (USA – Black American) – sculptor • **Celia Cruz** (Cuba) – salsa dancer • **Ester Mahlangu** (South Africa) – large-scale contemporary painter • **Fernando Botero** (Colombia) – figurative artist and sculptor • **Frida Kahlo** (Mexico) – painter • **Jacob Lawrence** (USA – Black American) – painter and large-scale muralist • **Jung Lee** (South Korea) – photographer • **Lloyd Kiva New** (USA – Native American) – printed textiles fashion designer • **Xeme** (Hong Kong) – graffiti artist

Mathematics	Connect math to the real world so students can be more interested, practice outside of school, and use it in their real lives. Use examples that students can connect with such as the price of a video gaming console, or going to amusement parks. Design lessons where students must notate prices of items at stores in their community and then use the examples to practice determining how much change they should receive. Geometry can be taught by asking students to think about how many family members are in their homes. For example, if a student lives with their mother, grandmother, and one sibling, you can explain that they are 1/4 of their household.
Music & Dance	• Do not show mainstream American pop music as the norm, and other music genres are subtypes of music • Explore different types of musical genres with students • Explain connections between rock, jazz, and hip-hop • Show students instruments from around the world and how they are connected to different cultures • Provide examples of Black country artists, White R&B artists, and Latinx jazz artists • Highlight different types of dance and their origins: rumba, ballet, tap, jazz, hip-hop, modern, break, and folk
Science	As you teach about topics related to science, include scientists of color who have contributed to the field. For example, you could expose students to • **Archaeology** (Bertha Parker Pallan Cody - Native American) • **Agricultural Science** (George Washington Carver - Black American) • **Chemistry** (Dr. Ahmed Hassan Zewail - Arab American) • **Engineering** (Mary Golda Ross - Native American) • **Viral Immunology** (Dr. Kizzmekia Corbett - Black American) • **Virology** (Dr. Flossie Wong-Staal - Asian American)
Social Studies	The potential is endless for showing cultures within the country and around the world. You can do this when teaching: • **Civics and Government**: Different government structures within the country and around the world. Explain how citizenship is defined, and illustrate how certain groups have been historically treated as second-class citizens based on the demographic group they were born into. This is another place where you can talk about Dr. Martin Luther King, Jr. and Rosa Parks. • **Culture and Society**: Collect and locate oral histories of cultures from within the country and around the world. Show students artifacts and symbols that are associated with different cultures. Religions and associated holidays and customs could be included in this curriculum. • **Economics**: Explain different economic structures, industries, taxes, and employment opportunities. Break down the system of the economy and how economics from around the world interact with and influence each other. • **Geography**: Explore different lands, places, regions, locations, landforms, and movements that represent the rich and diverse people and cultures from around the world.

INCORPORATING ANTI-RACIST CURRICULUM

It might not come as a surprise to you that to plan for anti-bias instruction you need to use an anti-racist curriculum. In Chapter 7, we discussed building an anti-racist culture as well as the impact of equity-mindedness and anti-racist teaching in DELE. Now that you have started to shift your mindset toward equity and established some ideas for anti-bias instruction, think about incorporating an anti-racist curriculum.

Scan this QR code to view anti-racist learning plans from Learning for Justice.

The Learning for Justice organization, formerly Tolerance.org, has created a series of anti-racist learning plans geared toward K–12 students. The lesson plans are linked to Common Core Standards, specific subject areas, grade bands, and social justice domains. As you develop your own anti-racist teaching practices, we encourage you to also provide your students with the same knowledge, awareness, and skills. To access the anti-racist learning plans, scan this QR code.

Not only is it important for us as teachers to develop anti-racist attitudes, but it is also our duty to help our students see the world through a just and equitable lens. Students are impressionable and, as teachers, we are in positions of power and influence. Similar to the ways in which the media influences students' thinking and perpetuates stereotypes they bring to school toward their peers, we can have a powerful impact on helping students see how institutionalized racism has negatively impacted educational environments. According to Kehoe (1994), as we teach students through an anti-racism lens, we help students develop their own anti-racist viewpoints when we give them the opportunities to:

1. Discuss past and present racism, stereotyping, and discrimination in society.

2. Learn the economic structural and historical roots of inequality.

3. Find examples of institutional racism in the school and confront them (confronting might include informing the administration or protesting).

4. Analyze unequal social and power relations.

5. Know the realities of racism and know the human consequences of racism.

6. Try to change the unequal social realities that are justified by racist ideology, but which can be changed by legislative or other action. (p. 355)

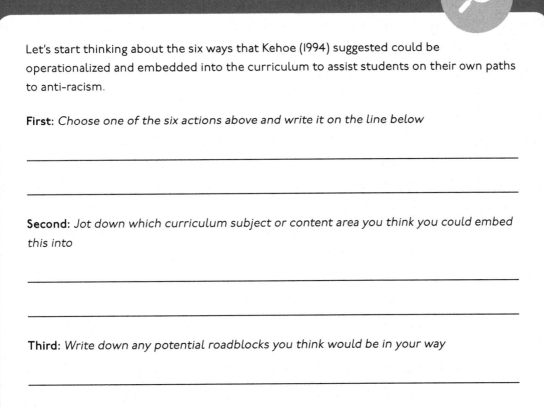

ANTI-BIAS EXERCISE 8.2

Let's start thinking about the six ways that Kehoe (1994) suggested could be operationalized and embedded into the curriculum to assist students on their own paths to anti-racism.

First: *Choose one of the six actions above and write it on the line below*

_____

_____

Second: *Jot down which curriculum subject or content area you think you could embed this into*

_____

_____

Third: *Write down any potential roadblocks you think would be in your way*

_____

_____

TWO SIDES TO EVERY STORY: HONORING MULTIPLE VIEWPOINTS

Often, two people can experience the same event but leave with a different viewpoint of what exactly happened. While there may be some similarities between stories, the old saying that *there is one side, the other side, and then the truth*, often rings true. Most of what we teach in the classroom is no different than this. The books we use for curriculum materials are written by authors who have their own point of view, that are based on the experiences they have had in their lives, who they are and how they identify, and the demographic and cultural groups they belong to. The same goes for the video materials we use, projects we design, stories we tell, and even historical "facts" we share. Because of this, "educators must also include viewpoints and narratives that have not been part of 'traditional' course materials" (Bass & Lawrence-Riddel, 2020, para. 5).

Scan this QR code to view UNC's Culturally Responsive Library Walk template.

As you develop course content and locate curriculum materials for your classes, ensure that they are filled with diverse voices and perspectives. Do not rely on the same types of authors who have had similar experiences. Include the voices of people from different ethnicities, nationalities, genders, and abilities. Introduce students to LGBT families and women and men in nontraditional careers. Also, when you are teaching history, include the perspectives of the different groups that were impacted. UNC's School of Information and Library Science has a Culturally Responsive Library Walk template that can be used by educators to assess whether your school's library is prepared to address the needs of Black students. Scan the QR code to access the template. Although the template was designed with Black students in mind, it can be used for all different students as you look at the strengths and gaps of your library materials regarding cultural responsiveness.

As you think more closely about the ways to consider multiple perspectives in your culturally responsive teaching, look over Table 8.2, which provides an example of a template you could use when teaching about the Women's Suffrage movement.

Table 8.2 • Multiple Viewpoints Book Review Template

TOPIC	WOMEN'S SUFFRAGE MOVEMENT		
NAME OF BOOK			
MAIN IDEA			
VIEWPOINTS OF MAIN CHARACTERS *(There is always more than one perspective, and each person and/or group of people have different shared experiences. Think about what you have learned about women, men, and the government during the Women's Suffrage movement. Consider intersectional identities and experiences such as those of Black women, Indigenous women, Black men, Indigenous men, etc. Respond to the questions below as related to each group.)*			
	WOMEN	**MEN**	**GOVERNMENT**
How did each group view the Women's Suffrage movement?			
From their perspective, why did each group support or oppose the Women's Suffrage movement?			
How would the women gaining the same voting rights as men impact each group?			
Is there anything else helpful to note about each group's perspective regarding this issue?			

CONTEXTUALIZING LEARNING: EXPOSING STUDENTS TO DIVERSE CULTURES

An important piece of anti-bias instruction is to provide students with the opportunity to see themselves in the curriculum, to connect learning with students' identities, and to expose students to other peoples, cultures, and the larger world. Learning must be contextualized in a way that makes it seamless for students to connect with, engage in, and benefit from regarding their overall learning. While putting learning in the context of the lived experiences of students, we must be mindful of the hidden curriculum; those "expectations, skill sets, knowledge, and social process[es] can help or hinder student achievement and belief systems. A hidden curriculum refers to the unspoken or implicit values, behaviors, procedures, and norms that exist in the educational setting" (Alsubaie, 2015, p. 125). We must be cognizant of those informal, yet impactful messages that we send students that may be attached to our own values, perspectives, and lived experiences but not with our students. For example, grading expectations, cultural norms in the classroom, and how we deliver feedback to students need to be explicit, explained, and done with a specific culture in mind.

Within Online Learning Settings

Technology and the increase of available tools to support online learning have created many pathways to assist teachers in contextualizing learning for students.

- **Augmented and Virtual Reality:** Students often are taught about historical places and events within the United States and around the world. Many times, these revolve heavily around the American Revolution, different domestic wars, and the acquisition of land from the dominant perspective. Within the United States, there are many other cultures and students can use the internet and any compatible device to virtually explore historical events, figures, art movements, and places around the globe through Google Arts & Cultures. There are also dozens of interactive experiments that are connected to different subject areas, environments around the world, and cultures that students can interact with.

Scan this QR code to view the Google Arts & Culture website.

- **Virtual Museum Tours:** There are excellent and enriching museums around the world; however, we cannot expose our students to them due to geographical constraints. Over the past several years, museums around the world have offered virtual tours via the

Scan this QR code to access the virtual tour of the Louvre Museum in Paris.

Scan this QR code to access the virtual tour of the Alaska Native Heritage Center in Anchorage.

Scan this QR code to access the virtual tour of the African art collection at the Metropolitan Museum of Art in New York.

internet. When teaching students about France, French cultures, or even Italian artists such as Leonardo da Vinci who painted the Mona Lisa, you can take your students to the Louvre Museum in Paris. Or when you are teaching about the history of Native Americans and Pacific Islanders or the state of Alaska, you can bring your students through the Alaska Native Heritage Center. When teaching about different cultures within the continent of Africa and related cultural artifacts, a trip to the Metropolitan Museum of Art in New York's virtual African art collection can complement your culturally responsive and anti-bias lessons.

Within In-Person Learning Settings

In-person learning opportunities present different ways for students to collaborate, inquire, and build their own knowledge and awareness of the world around them.

- **Meaningful Makerspaces:** A makerspace is "a place where young people have an opportunity to explore their own interests; learn to use tools and materials both physical and virtual; and develop creative projects" (Fleming, 2015, p. 5). The types of projects that can be created in makerspaces are endless. Instead of assigning students to create one type of bridge or an airplane, a makerspace can be used to allow students to create based on their own thinking, perspectives, and experiences. There is always more than one way to solve problems. In one student's household, they may boil water on the stove for tea while other households may heat the water in the microwave. The same goes for building, making, and creating within makerspaces. Projects in makerspaces can be open and rubrics for assessments can be designed based on the process, not the product. Students' ways of doing and making, which are influenced by who they are and the cultural values they bring to the class, should be honored. Remember, one way of heating water is not superior to the other just as one way of *making* is not. Within a makerspace, there is an opportunity to demonstrate to students just that.

- **Project-Based Learning:** The Buck Institute for Education PBL Works (2021) describes Project-Based Learning (PBL) as "a teaching method in which students learn by actively engaging in real-world and personally meaningful projects" (para. 1). PBL can be based on any subject area and the topic and focus options are endless. For a culturally responsive classroom especially, this means that students can choose their own topics and projects can be based on their interests. As the teacher, you can encourage students to draw on their cultural assets, community, and lived experiences to enhance their projects. PBL also provides the opportunity for students to work collaboratively with and learn from each other.

ANTI-BIAS EXERCISE 8.3

Stop and Reflect by responding to the following:

What specific pedagogical practices have you previously employed to expose your students to diverse cultures, perspectives, and points of view?

_____

_____

What are you hoping to try for the first time?

_____

_____

WHAT'S NEXT?

We hope you have a better understanding of what anti-bias instruction is, its relation to culturally responsive teaching, and how to plan for it. Now that you have spent time thinking about the ways in which you can include multiple viewpoints and perspectives in your teaching, and tap into your students' unique backgrounds and talents, you are well positioned to implement anti-bias instruction in your own DELE. Before you move on to Chapter 9, complete the reflection questions below to see how your understanding and perspectives have changed around anti-bias instruction and use this chapter's culturally sustaining checklist and action plan to support your plan for incorporating the content in this chapter within your culturally responsive teaching practices.

REFLECTION QUESTIONS

You have worked through Chapter 8 and explored ways to plan and implement anti-bias instruction. Take a few minutes to read through and reflect on the reflection questions below. They may seem familiar because they are variations of the ones you completed prior to reading this chapter. Once you have recorded your responses, go back to the beginning of the chapter to see how your knowledge, awareness, and skills surrounding anti-bias instruction have expanded.

- To my understanding, what is anti-bias instruction?

- How do I include the lived experiences and cultures of all students in class, beyond heroes and holidays?

- Why is it important to include multiple viewpoints when teaching?

- What did I learn from this chapter?

_____

_____

_____

_____

_____

_____

_____

_____

_____

_____

_____

Appendix 8.1

Culturally Sustaining Checklist: Preparing for Anti-Bias Instruction

On a scale of 1–4, please select how much you agree or disagree with the following statements.

1 = Strongly Disagree	2 = Disagree	3 = Agree	4 = Strongly Agree

ON A SCALE OF 1–4, INDICATE YOUR LEVEL OF AWARENESS.	AWARENESS	NOTES FOR FURTHER DEVELOPMENT:
	I am aware of what anti-bias instruction is.	
	I am aware that I can plan for anti-bias instruction.	
	I am aware that anti-bias instruction can contribute to DELE.	
ON A SCALE OF 1–4, INDICATE YOUR LEVEL OF KNOWLEDGE.	KNOWLEDGE	NOTES FOR FURTHER DEVELOPMENT:
	I know how to describe anti-bias instruction.	
	I know why culturally responsive teaching must go beyond heroes and holidays.	
	I know the value of bringing in multiple perspectives when teaching content to students.	
ON A SCALE OF 1–4, INDICATE YOUR LEVEL OF SKILL.	SKILLS	NOTES FOR FURTHER DEVELOPMENT:
	I can plan for anti-bias instruction.	
	I can locate the appropriate curriculum required for anti-bias instruction.	
	I can implement anti-bias instruction.	

Appendix 8.2

Action Plan: How Will I Plan and Implement Anti-Bias Instruction?

What are three actions you can take to use what you have learned in this chapter to plan and implement anti-bias instruction?

1.

2.

3.

What supports or information do you need to successfully complete the three actions you listed above?

1.

2.

3.

What challenges and barriers do you expect to be faced with in carrying out the three actions you listed above, and what ideas do you have for addressing them?

CHALLENGES/BARRIERS	IDEAS TO ADDRESS THEM
1.	
2.	
3.	

How do you expect your students to benefit from you taking the three actions listed above?

_____

_____

_____

Appendix 8.3   Responsive Resources

Scan the QR codes below to access the following resources as you continue to learn about planning for anti-bias instruction.

RESOURCE TYPE	TITLE	URL
Article	"Social Justice and Anti-Bias Instruction" *(The IDEAL School of Manhattan)*	
Book	*Not Light but Fire: How to Lead Meaningful Race Conversations in the Classroom* by Matthew R. Kay (Stenhouse)	
Podcast	Teaching Hard History	
Video	"Teaching Tolerance Anti-Bias Framework" (Gary Gray)	

CHAPTER NINE

Preparing Culturally Responsive Authentic Assessments

REFLECTION QUESTIONS

Before delving into the chapter's contents, take a few minutes to work through the following reflection questions. There is space provided below for your responses. We revisit variations of these reflection questions at the end of the chapter.

- How are culturally responsive teaching and assessment practices related?

- Why is it important to ensure that assessments are culturally relevant?

- What are some of the current issues related to cultural bias and standardized assessments?

- What types of alternative and authentic assessments could I create to align with a culturally responsive classroom culture?

- What do I hope to learn from this chapter?

_____

_____

_____

_____

_____

THE *WHAT* AND *WHY* OF ASSESSMENTS

This chapter brings us to the final chapter of the book and is focused on creating culturally responsive authentic assessments for all our students. Assessment is a broad term that can be described as a "wide variety of methods or tools that educators use to evaluate, measure, and document the academic readiness, learning progress, skill acquisition, or educational needs of students" (Glossary of Education Reform, 2015, para. 1). We must have fair and equitable mechanisms to determine that our students are learning, growing, and developing as a result of our instruction.

We learned in Chapter 8 how to curate culturally relevant curriculum materials and teach students in ways that speak to their learning styles, backgrounds, and from varied perspectives that they can connect with. In the same vein, we must assess the learning that has taken place within our culturally relevant classrooms. Simply put, we need to know that our culturally responsive teaching is effective. This can also be done if the assessments we create are accessible, equitable, and not created with one group in mind. Assessment in the 21st century looks different than it did in the past. We are preparing students for positions that have not previously existed and are focusing not only on academic content but also on students' ability to critically think, communicate, collaborate, and use their creative skills (Budhai & Taddei, 2015).

In this chapter, we provide you with strategies and tools that can be leveraged as you create culturally responsive authentic assessments that are aligned with Dynamic Equitable Learning Environments (DELE):

- Discussing the critical need for culturally responsive assessments in K–12 teaching and learning environments

- Highlighting the dangers of biased language and content within standardized assessments

- Describing the ways that assessments can be crafted to tap into students' unique and diverse backgrounds

- Reviewing a variety of authentic assessments that can contextualize learning for students

While reading through this chapter's content, we hope you continuously think about your own assessment practices and how they can be reimagined to include some of the constructs of culturally responsive pedagogy. This chapter includes myriad of assessment ideas, and we encourage you to take notes in the spaces provided for this chapter's Anti-Bias Exercises so you can come back to them during the school year as needed.

THE NECESSITY OF CULTURALLY RESPONSIVE ASSESSMENTS

In agreement with Slee (2010), we cannot evaluate students using a standard set of outcomes. Instead, we must allow students to demonstrate their knowledge in culturally relevant and responsive ways. Similar to what we discussed in Chapter 8, curriculum and instruction must connect to the lived experiences, perspectives, and values of each student. If we conduct our classroom teaching in this way, through the lens of culturally responsive teaching, then the ways in which we assess students must be similar.

Validity: Validity is "the quality of a test; the degree to which an instrument measures what it was designed to measure" (Overton, 2012, p. 124). We assess students to "find out what students have learned, to hold them accountable, and to help guide and set the pace for the classroom" (Gibson, 2020, para. 5). If students are being assessed on content that they have not learned, that they have not been exposed to, or that requires prerequisite knowledge they would only have through a social context based on being part of a certain racial, ethnic, cultural, social, and/or economic demographic group, then the validity of the assessment is compromised.

Interest: Assessments, while seemingly a mundane experience, do not have to be stagnant for students. We can create assessments for students that they are interested in and connect to the world around them. Lynch (2016) shares in an *Education Week* opinion article ideas for creating culturally responsive assessments that speak to the lived experiences of students in different settings by suggesting:

> An inner city math teacher, for example, could tweak his tests with word problems that best relate to the students entering his classroom and not use obscure references that make the material seem even more disconnected from the real life of the students. A science teacher at an elite prep school could do the same, using references that strike a chord with the students who walk through the door and grounding the material. (para. 2)

These suggestions are a starting point and bring to life the point that as teachers, we need to get to know our students (Chapter 5), families and communities (Chapter 6), and to use the information to tweak assessments so they are not only culturally relevant but also fair and actually test students on what they have actually learned. It is important to note that while the examples above provide two different settings (inner city and elite prep school), it is quite possible for an elite prep school to be located within an inner city and/or the students within the inner city school may have very different experiences from one another. As we respond to the cultural needs of students, we must do so in a way that values and acknowledges the individuality of students within the same demographic group. We must always look at and treat students as individuals and assess their learning accordingly.

ANTI-BIAS EXERCISE 9.1

Stop and reflect here. We briefly touch on the critical need to have culturally responsive assessments. Think back about assessments you have given in the past; would you consider them culturally relevant? Share details below about why or why not.

_____

_____

_____

TEACHER-MADE AND CURRICULUM-BASED ASSESSMENTS

There are different types of assessments including benchmark, diagnostic, norm-referenced, formative, and summative. Benchmark assessments are typically administered throughout the school year to check in and determine if students are making progress toward meeting grade-level standards. Diagnostic and norm-referenced assessments are more standardized and are usually monitored through the state and federal governments for public schools, and other governing boards for private schools. For the purposes of this book, we are primarily focusing on formative and summative assessments, although there is a section below with pertinent information on bias in intelligence and standardized assessments that teachers should be cognizant of.

According to Duckor (2017), "formative evaluation occurs during the learning, summative at the end of the marking period" (p. xvii). Formative assessments can actually occur before, during, and after the lesson. Formative assessments are an important aspect of any classroom community because it provides teachers with information that can be used to guide their teaching practice. On the other hand, summative assessments are typically given at the end of a unit or marking period. The information that formative and summative assessments provide teachers with are the skills acquired by students and how much learning has occurred over a set period of time.

Formative and summative assessments usually have letter or numerical grades associated with the results. These grades are then the basis of students' report cards and permanent records that are used for students to obtain entry into special admission high schools and colleges. Because of this, formative and summative assessments must be created in culturally responsive ways. Students should know what they are being assessed on, and the questions should be written in a way that is geared toward varied and diverse sets of perspectives and worldviews. Formative and summative assessments should also go beyond the traditional assessment methods, leveraging authentic ways for students to engage in the assessment process.

A CAUTION REGARDING BIASED INTELLIGENCE AND STANDARDIZED TESTING

While we want you to gain strategies and ideas to create culturally responsive authentic assessments for those that we as teachers generally have direct control and influence over regarding the content, it is still imperative to recognize the reality of biased questioning within intelligence and standardized testing. There is a long-standing history in the United States of intelligence tests being culturally biased and geared toward students who are part of the majority group (Franklin, 2007).

A social psychologist and researcher at Stanford University, Steele (1999), provided expert witness testimony in the *Gratz et al. v Bollinger et al.* and *Grutter et al. v Bollinger* cases stating:

> Many factors including heredity may underlie scholastic aptitude, but even the highest estimates of hereditary influence allow for substantial influence of experiential factors. This means that one's performance on these tests can be influenced by one's experience, by one's cultural background, by one's access to schooling and the cultural perspectives, attitudes, and know-hows that might favor test performance by the extent to which one's peers value school achievement, by the nature of one's dinner table conversation, and so on. (p. 411)

There is myriad contributing school, teacher-centered, student-centered, local community, and family factors that have influenced the achievement gap between White and Black students regarding standardized testing

Scan this QR code to watch a video of Dr. Ibram X. Kendi titled "How standardized tests were designed by racists and eugenicists."

performance (Arbuthnot, 2011). These include, but are not limited to, academic rigor, tracking, teacher experience, cultural sensitivity, access to child care, social services, after school programs, stereotype threat (Chapter 4), self-efficacy, socioeconomic status, home environment, and primary home language (Arbuthnot, 2011).

Dr. Ibram X Kendi, the author of *How to be an Anti-Racist*, discusses more on the background around how standardized tests were created in intentionally biased ways. Scan the QR to view the video. After viewing the video, complete Anti-Bias Exercise 9.2 below.

ANTI-BIAS EXERCISE 9.2

We just went over issues related to bias in intelligence and standardized tests. Think back to when you took standardized tests or to your past experience delivering standardized testing to students. Complete the table below to the best of your memory, based on your past experiences. You can do one or both of the examples below, depending on your experiences.

TYPE OF ASSESSMENTS	INTELLIGENCE	STANDARDIZED
Name of the intelligence or standardized test.		
What grade/age levels was the test created for?		
What words, questions, or phrasing seemed to be geared toward the majority population?		
How could the intelligence and/or standardized test be modified to be more culturally relevant to a larger group of students?		

OFFERING CULTURALLY RELEVANT ALTERNATIVE ASSESSMENTS

Instead of trying to fit culturally and linguistically diverse students into existing assessments, to be culturally responsive to their unique needs means considering different forms of assessment types beyond traditional tests (Laher & Cockcroft, 2017). Remember, there is always more than one way to achieve the same goal, and the same is true for assessing student learning. Imagine that you are teaching a fifth-grade geometry lesson on degrees of angles and have created a formative assessment where students must illustrate that they understand how many degrees each angle is. Instead of providing students only one option for this assessment, in this case, you ask students to draw the angle using paper and pencil, what if you allow students to use an online drawing tool or physical manipulatives, or create a video where they move their own body parts to show the correct angle? This is all part of being culturally responsive to the unique skill sets, interests, and perspectives of your students when developing varied assessment types for them.

Not only is offering options for alternative assessments a part of culturally responsive teaching, but it is also a way to differentiate instruction (Tomlinson, 1995) to meet the unique learning needs of each student. And, it helps students connect with their strengths and intelligences that they are strongest in (Gardner, 2006). Some students may be better positioned to articulate their point of view through a debate or responding to a case study while others may benefit by creating a digital mind map or online Venn diagram. If you can, go back to Chapter 4 where we discussed cultural capital and the Community Cultural Wealth Model (Yosso, 2005). As you develop culturally responsive assessments for students, think about these concepts and how you can provide students with opportunities to show you what they know, in ways that would leverage the assets they bring into the classroom.

ANTI-BIAS EXERCISE 9.3

Look at the list of potential assessment types. Jot down next to each assessment type one way you could craft the assessment to connect to each students' unique and diverse backgrounds and lived experiences. Also, provide a short rationale surrounding your thinking.

(Continued)

(Continued)

ASSESSMENT TYPE	BRIEF DESCRIPTION OF ALTERNATIVE	RATIONALE
Written paper	Offer students the option to develop a podcast where they would share responses to a prompt orally instead of writing a traditional paper.	The student may be from a culture that values oral communication and has received practice in it over the years.
Math word problem		
Test or quiz		

EQUITABLE EXPERIENTIAL AND INCLUSIVE INQUIRY-BASED AUTHENTIC ASSESSMENTS

To ensure that assessment practices are equitable, we must go beyond traditional assessments that are created with one dominant group in mind. Since standardized assessments are developed with cultural, racial, and socioeconomic bias, performance-based assessments such as capstones, portfolios, and public exhibitions offer diverse students the chance to demonstrate their knowledge on a topic connected to their identity, which impacts their overall growth and development (Choi, 2020). By leveraging experiential and inquiry-based learning, students from diverse backgrounds can demonstrate their knowledge while leveraging their cultural assets, lived experiences, and unique perspectives. In addition, students can work in concert with each other, and lead projects that they are interested in, while showing us as the teacher what they know.

Vygotsky (1978) has published many educational theories surrounding the influence that social contexts can have on the process of learning, along with the impact one's culture has on how they acquire knowledge. Instead of solely relying on culturally biased tests and quizzes to assess student learning, experiential and inquiry-based learning assessments can be exploited to provide all students with more equitable opportunities to demonstrate their knowledge. In fact:

[o]ne powerful means of bringing students' culture into the classroom is through culturally relevant performance assessments. Performance assessments center students' identity and experiences by asking them to show what they know and can do through multidisciplinary projects, presentations of their learning in front of a panel, and reflections on their educational trajectory. At their core, such assessments provide a critical space for students to reflect on and share their personal stories and their identities as learners. (Kaul, 2019, para. 2)

A few types of performance and experiential learning assessments are:

Capstone Projects: A capstone project is a culminating, summative assessment that can take a wide variety of formats. Some capstones may be a formal writing research project while others may be a presentation of comprehensive materials studied. Instead of having one type of capstone project, in culturally responsive classrooms, students should be encouraged to choose topics that have relevance to the context they lived in and should be able to use the experiences they had within the project. Teachers and students can meet to plan the capstone project and determine what the student is interested in. Prior to the start of the capstone projects, students should be given a preference inventory that can be completed to help them discover some of their interests. Specific skills can and should be assessed that the students have met, but the type of and how they carry out the capstone project should be open.

Makerspace Inquiry: A makerspace, which is a learning space with a variety of tools, materials, and textiles, provides students the opportunity to discover and explore items they are interested in (Fleming, 2015). Within a makerspace, students can be challenged to solve societal problems collectively, while demonstrating their competencies with critical thinking, communication, collaboration, and creativity. Culturally responsive assessment activities can be developed within a makerspace, and teachers should ensure their students' identities, along ethnically and culturally diverse content and materials, are included within makerspace experiences (Kye, 2020).

Portfolios: Portfolios are a combination of learning artifacts that students have created through a term or school year. Portfolios can include interdisciplinary content or focus specifically on one content area. To gauge and assess students' critical thinking and achievement of deeper learning (Wren, 2019), a presentation surrounding the artifacts within the portfolio could be part of the portfolio requirements. Even well put together portfolios may benefit from an explanation from students surrounding their thinking and how they came to develop each artifact. Because each student will have unique lived experiences and see the world based on their social context, a presentation of portfolios can help teachers understand how students have not only come to acquire knowledge but also how they have applied it in other contexts.

Service-Learning Projects: Service-learning is a "form of experiential education in which learners engage in activities that address human and community needs together with structured opportunities intentionally designed to promote student learning and development" (Jacoby, 1999, p. 20). Service-learning is distinct from community service because it includes reflection and is directly connected to academic content. Service-learning projects can be created for any academic discipline. When students engage in service-learning projects, they develop an understanding of realities within the larger society and learn more about other communities (Budhai, 2013). Service-learning can provide an authentic culturally responsive assessment opportunity for students and can serve as an alternative way for students to demonstrate their knowledge while participating in civic engagement efforts, and can help develop their multicultural competence (Borden, 2007).

Table 9.1 • Examples of Equitable Experiential and Inclusive Inquiry-Based Assessments That Can Be Used in Online and In-Person Learning Environments

TYPE OF CULTURALLY RELEVANT ASSESSMENT	SKILLS ASSESSED	WHAT IT "LOOKS" ONLINE	WHAT IT "LOOKS" IN PERSON
Capstone projects	Information literacy, research, and the ability to organize and put together a body of content in a cohesive and concise manner.	Students completing online courses could leverage the resources of the community such as the library as well as digital repositories available by the school to support content for their projects. The teacher or an advisor for middle and high school students should be available to meet virtually with students and check in on their progress with their capstones.	In-person students will have available the school library as well as online databases with content. Even though students will be learning in person, some of the work they will complete for the capstone project may be completed outside of traditional class time. Students should stay connected with the teacher either before or after class, or schedule progress monitoring meetings to ensure appropriate progress is being made.
Makerspace inquiry	In addition to assessing students' content knowledge such as spatial reasoning and computational	While learning online, students could use a makerspace area within their home that uses inexpensive everyday products that would otherwise be recycled or	Students can engage in the makerspace physically in person at school. Makerspaces could be available in the school as an independent room or a special area within the

TYPE OF CULTURALLY RELEVANT ASSESSMENT	SKILLS ASSESSED	WHAT IT "LOOKS" ONLINE	WHAT IT "LOOKS" IN PERSON
	skills, makerspaces can assess students' 21st century skills. For example, makerspaces can also be used to assess soft skills such as problem-solving, agency, creativity, and collaboration (Chang, 2018).	trashed (Taddei & Budhai, 2017). Students can also use culturally relevant artifacts that are found in their homes such as instruments, artwork, utensils, and textiles to inspire their creativity and inquiry process.	physical classroom. Teachers should make sure that the materials within makerspaces are culturally relevant to all students.
Portfolios	Portfolios can be used to document student progress each term, throughout the year, or on a specific set of competencies. This can be anything from oral and writing samples from English Language Arts classes, science experimentations write-up and lab sheets, or historical documents and assignments as related to social studies course content. Create broad rubrics without specificity on the types of products that are needed to ensure that students can cultivate a diverse set of artifacts.	Students who are completing portfolios can choose a digital curation tool such as Wakelet or Google Sites to house their digital portfolios. To easily share their work with other teachers, administrators, and families, a QR code could be given to the student that can take others directly to their portfolio, or a URL can be shared.	Students who are learning in person can also benefit from having a digital portfolio. Some teachers still prefer having a physical binder; however, that can be used as an artifact within the classroom library and space. When meeting with parents about student progress, the portfolio can support the verbal narrative and information we as teachers provide to families about their children's assessment and overall learning progress.
Service-learning projects	The skills assessed in a service-learning project will relate to the corresponding project in the respective class. For example, to assess students' understanding fluency and language acquisition in a foreign language course, they could work with a community organization by translating flyers for community members. Or students studying environmental science can work with a local arboretum to properly take care of trees.	In an online class, students will carry out the service portion of their service-learning project at a community organization. However, they will attend classes virtually. Students can use an online tool such as VoiceThread to reflect on their service experience and make connections to course content. Classmates and teachers can go onto VoiceThread to listen to the students' reflections and leave comments.	In an in-person class, students will also carry out the service portion of their service-learning project at a community organization. However, they will attend classes physically at the school. Students can reflect on their service experience and share their learning orally with the other students in the class.

Scan this QR code
to visit Rubric Maker,
where you can create
a custom rubric
template.

All the assessment activities noted in Table 9.1 should be accompanied by a rubric. The rubric will have the skills and content you are assessing students on listed in the far left column, and in the top row will be the level of competence. By using customizable rubric templates through a site such as Rubric Maker, you can adjust the rubrics based on each particular assessment and the constructs of learning that students are focusing on. Scan the QR code to try out Rubric Maker as you develop equitable experiential and inclusive inquiry-based assessments. Because you are creating customized rubrics as opposed to using generic ones, you can add in aspects of cultural competence, student interests, and other areas related to culturally relevant assessment practices.

WHAT'S NEXT?

This chapter concludes the content surrounding culturally responsive teaching online and in person, and brings us to the conclusion of this book. In Part I, we uncovered any unconscious, implicit and explicit biases that we may bring to the classroom as well as worked through strategies for eliminating microaggressions. In Part II, we explored assets-based teaching approaches and ways to develop the whole student, while drawing on their strengths. We also discussed ways to connect with students' families and communities in an effort to positively impact their overall learning experiences and maximize each students' cultural capital. In Part III, we laid the groundwork for creating equity-mindedness and decolonizing the classroom environment. We also highlighted ways to incorporate culturally relevant curriculum and content into the classroom that both touch on students' diverse lived experiences, and also come from different perspectives.

At the end of this book, there is an epilogue that serves as a call to action for you. We hope you will use all the strategies, content, techniques, and skills to not only employ culturally responsive teaching practices in your own online and in-person classrooms, but also impact your school, school district, and the larger society. Before you move to read through the epilogue, we encourage you to complete the reflection questions below to see how your thinking has changed around preparing culturally responsive authentic assessments and use this chapter's culturally sustaining checklist and action plan to support your plan for incorporating the content in this chapter within your culturally responsive teaching practices.

REFLECTION QUESTIONS

You have worked through Chapter 9 and explored ways to prepare culturally relevant assessments for online and in-person learning environments. Take a few minutes to read through and reflect on the reflection questions below. They may seem familiar because they are variations of the ones you completed prior to reading this chapter. Once you have recorded your responses, go back to the beginning of the chapter to see how your knowledge, awareness, and skills surrounding culturally responsive authentic assessments have expanded.

- What does it mean to have a culturally relevant assessment?

- How can I ensure that the assessments I create are culturally relevant?

- What can I do to address some of the current issues related to cultural bias and standardized assessments?

- What types of alternative and authentic assessments could I create to align with a culturally responsive classroom culture?

- What did I learn from this chapter?

_____

_____

_____

_____

_____

_____

_____

_____

Appendix 9.1

Culturally Sustaining Checklist: Culturally Responsive Assessments

On a scale of 1–4, please select how much you agree or disagree with the following statements.

1 = Strongly Disagree   2 = Disagree   3 = Agree   4 = Strongly Agree

ON A SCALE OF 1–4, INDICATE YOUR LEVEL OF AWARENESS.	AWARENESS	NOTES FOR FURTHER DEVELOPMENT:
	I am aware of what a culturally relevant assessment is.	
	I am aware that part of being a culturally responsive educator is to ensure that assessments are unbiased.	
	I am aware of the biased language in standardized assessments.	

ON A SCALE OF 1–4, INDICATE YOUR LEVEL OF KNOWLEDGE.	KNOWLEDGE	NOTES FOR FURTHER DEVELOPMENT:
	I know the teacher's role in creating culturally relevant assessments.	
	I know the importance of using alternative assessments to support culturally and linguistically diverse students.	
	I know that a general rubric should be used to assess student performance on authentic assessments.	

ON A SCALE OF 1–4, INDICATE YOUR LEVEL OF SKILL.	SKILLS	NOTES FOR FURTHER DEVELOPMENT:
	I can articulate the ways in which assessments can be biased.	
	I can offer students alternative culturally relevant assessments.	
	I can include equitable experiential and inquiry-based authentic assessments in my classes.	

Appendix 9.2

Action Plan: How Will I Create Culturally Responsive and Relevant Authentic Assessments in Online and In-Person Learning Environments?

What are three actions you can take to use what you have learned in this chapter to prepare culturally responsive and relevant authentic assessments in online and in-person learning environments?

1.

2.

3.

What supports or information do you need to successfully complete the three actions you listed above?

1.

2.

3.

What challenges and barriers do you expect to be faced with in carrying out the three actions you listed above, and what ideas do you have for addressing them?

CHALLENGES/BARRIERS	IDEAS TO ADDRESS THEM
1.	
2.	
3.	

How do you expect your students to benefit from you taking the three actions listed above?

_____

_____

_____

Appendix 9.3   Responsive Resources

Scan the QR codes to access the following resources as you continue to learn about developing culturally responsive assessments.

RESOURCE TYPE	TITLE	URL
Article	"Classroom Tips: Classroom Assessments for All Learners" by Laura Greenstein *(Phi Delta Kappan)*	
Microcredential	*Developing a Mindset for Culturally Responsive Assessment* (Digital Promise)	
Podcast	"Zaretta Hammond: What is Culturally-Responsive Teaching?" (The 180 Podcast)	
Video	Culturally Responsive Assessments (US PREP)	

Epilogue

A Call to Action

Leveraging One's Own Power and Privilege to Dismantle Systemic Barriers for Sustainable and Equitable Learning

We have covered myriad topics throughout this action planner regarding culturally responsive teaching online and in person in Dynamic Equitable Learning Environments (DELE), but now what?

Consider these questions:

- How can *I* use this information beyond my own classroom?
- How can *I* ensure that students beyond my classroom benefit from culturally responsive teaching practices in online and in-person learning environments?
- How can *I* lead efforts within my school, my district, and beyond?

As you think about your responses to the questions above, what follows are five sustainable and equitable actions that you can take to leverage your own power and privilege by joining in on efforts to break down and dismantle systemic, institutional, and socio-political barriers that many students face. These actions are not just *one and done* types of things like having a surface-level cultural fest with different types of foods representing countries around the world, or attending a 1-hour webinar on diversity and inclusion, and not using what was learned in your work. The actions suggested below should become part of your continued work as a culturally responsive educator. Doing these things consistently brings continuity to the process and can have a true impact on sustainable and equitable learning for all students.

SUSTAINABLE AND EQUITABLE ACTION #1

Commit to Approaching Teaching and Learning Through a Social Justice Lens

Please, do not stop with the end of this book! The end of this action planner is the start of your new pedagogical approach to teaching and learning. All the anti-racist exercises you completed can be translated into your teaching and the ways in which you provide students access to the curriculum moving forward. To do this efficiently, effectively, and most important, equitably, you must be committed to continuing this work throughout your time as an educator and beyond. Too often, we as educators are subjected to one-off professional development, or using a different *new* curriculum set every couple of years. While exposure to emerging topics and content in the field has value, culturally responsive teaching cannot be approached in this way. In all aspects of our pedagogical practice, we have to approach teaching and learning from a social justice lens. Educational opportunities must be equitable in all aspects.

To approach teaching and learning from a social justice lens, you can:

- Continue to reflect on your own bias and make a plan to mitigate it to ensure that it does not perpetuate into your Dynamic Equitable Learning Environments (DELE).

- Call out microaggressions, microinsults, and microassaults that you hear from other educators, students, and families, and explain what they are and why they are hurtful and dangerous, and not a part of your online and/or in-person learning environments.

- Identify spaces and places where certain groups of students may not be treated equitably, and work with the school administration to ameliorate the situation, so their learning is not impacted.

- Plan, instruct, and assess students by including their lived experiences, worldviews, values, and cultural assets. Always bring in multiple perspectives and account for historical tragedies that have an impact on today's achievement gap.

SUSTAINABLE AND EQUITABLE ACTION #2

Create and Join Professional Learning and Connection Communities

We cannot do this work alone. We cannot work in silos. One of the benefits of the ubiquitous nature of technology is that there are seamless opportunities to make meaningful connections with others who have shared interests. It is exciting to have the knowledge, awareness, and skills required to be culturally responsive educators. However, doing this work is a collective effort. Students come in contact with different teachers throughout their educational experiences. You may also be one of the only teachers or one of the first in your school building to go through this action planner. To continue to develop your skills, be available and willing to exchange ideas, and learn how other educators are interpreting the action planner's content and using the materials to create DELE.

You can also start your own Professional Learning and Connection Communities. You have the content knowledge and are now actively thinking about topics related to equity and social justice. You can use your voice to get others involved by:

- **Leveraging Social Media:** There are several free social media tools that offer virtual spaces for like-minded people to connect. Consider starting and leading a Culturally Responsive Educator Facebook group. Start with teachers in your school building and school district. As friends of friends on Facebook learn of the group, others will join. On Twitter, use the Hashtag #CRTinDELE to connect with other educators who have read this book. Tag @DrBudhai, too! (And remember to tweet us your asset maps—we'd love to see them!)

- **Facilitate a Book Study:** Introduce this action planner to your colleagues and facilitate a book study. You could even have the book study as part of the Facebook group's engagement activities.

- **Lead Professional Development:** You have knowledge to share. Think about speaking at one of your school's professional development sessions and share a few best practices you learned from this action planner with your colleagues.

SUSTAINABLE AND EQUITABLE ACTION #3

Refer Students and Their Families to Safe Spaces and Supports

Safe spaces and targeted supports can be difficult to locate within certain online and in-person learning environments. Dr. Beverly Daniel Tatum's best-selling book, *Why Are All the Black Kids Sitting Together in the Cafeteria?*, illuminates the need to have a space and community of comfort to deal with negative discriminatory experiences, particularly in schools. Dr. Beverly Daniel Tatum builds on that work in the *Assimilation Blues: Black Families in White Communities, Who Succeeds and Why*, which is focused on Black families navigating White communities. Both books can be found by accessing the QR code.

Scan this QR code to learn more about Dr. Beverly Daniel Tatum's books.

As you continue your journey toward culturally responsive teaching, think about spaces and supports for diverse student and family needs and work toward providing them within your school, school district, and surrounding community. Even beyond finding spaces for your cultural and linguistically diverse learners, also consider other student populations.

For example, when you think about bathroom facilities, are single-stall bathrooms available for transgender and nonbinary students and their families? Students with health and personal space concerns could also benefit from this type of bathroom facility set-up. How about supporting religious diversity beyond excusing students for missing school for religious holidays? While the Supreme Court has restrictions on mandated prayer and the teaching of it in public schools, the Constitution still grants rights of freedom of religious expression. Given this, think of spaces where students can practice their respective religions, faiths, and spiritual values.

Online spaces and supports would be useful for students in transition, migrant families, and military families. This list is not exhaustive, and there is much work in different areas of equity and justice to tackle. What has been shared already can, however, serve as a guide to get you started with action.

SUSTAINABLE AND EQUITABLE ACTION #4

Consistently Connect, Communicate, and Collaborate With the Community

As you learned through this action planner, culturally responsive teaching, whether online or in person, involves more than just you as the teacher and students. To be truly culturally responsive requires including the whole student, their identity, and lived experience in the fabric of teaching and learning. This includes not only the students' families but the larger community. The community is what surrounds the school as well as each students' community where they live. Think about our work on the Community Cultural Wealth model (Yosso, 2005) and the different cultural assets that students bring to school. In this vein, connect the school and students' community with curriculum and instruction. Leverage the community assets and bring them into your DELE to consistently connect students to the world around them, while expanding their content knowledge and perspectives.

SUSTAINABLE AND EQUITABLE ACTION #5

Use Your Privilege to Address Systemic Racism in Schools

Now that you are aware of the institutional racism that has perpetuated school communities for decades, it is time to use your privilege to work toward ending it. One action you can take in this regard is being active with legislation. Write to Congress and state representatives. Request funding and question inequitable distribution of funding. Attend school board meetings and highlight issues surrounding the achievement gap, disparities in teacher preparation, and dichotomous resources between schools based on student demographics. You have power and you have the privilege of not only knowing about the issues that exist but also having a pathway and voice to advocate for those who have been silenced. You have power; use it. This action is just the beginning. This work is not easy. But as Mellody Hobson says in her TED Talk, "We must be color brave." Scan QR code to watch the full presentation.

Scan this QR code to watch Mellody Hobson's TEDTalk titled "Color blind or color brave?"

In this type of work, no action is too small. Continue to think about your plans for using your privilege and what you learned from this action planner to build, nurture, and facilitate DELE for your students.

Thank you for starting this journey toward culturally responsive teaching in online and in-person learning environments with us. We hope that the content of this action planner will be useful to you as you create, nurture, and sustain DELE.

References

Akos, P., & Kretchmar, J. (2016). Gender and Ethnic bias in Letters of Recommendation: Considerations for School Counselors. *Professional School Counseling, 20*(1),102–114. https://doi.org/10.5330/1096-2409-20.1.102

Algava, A. (2016). Beyond child-centered constructivism: A call for culturally sustaining progressive pedagogy. *Occasional Paper Series, 2016*(35). https://educate.bankstreet.edu/occasional-paper-series/vol2016/iss35/5

Alsubaie, M. A. (2015). Hidden curriculum as one of current issue of curriculum. *Journal of Education and Practice, 6*(33), 125–128.

Annamma, S., & Morrison, D. (2018). Identifying dysfunctional education ecologies: A DisCrit analysis of bias in the classroom. *Equity & Excellence in Education, 51*(2), 114–131. https://doi.org/10.1080/10665684.2018.1496047

Arao, B., & Clemens, K. (2013). From safe spaces to brave spaces: A new way to frame dialogue around diversity and social justice. In L. M. Landreman (Ed.), *The art of effective facilitation: Reflections from social justice educators* (pp. 135–150). Stylus.

Arbuthnot, K. (2011). *Filling in the blanks: Standardized testing and the black-white achievement gap.* Information Age.

Baker, B. D., & Corcoran, S. P. (2012). *The stealth inequities of school funding: How state and local school finance systems perpetuate inequitable student spending.* Center for American Progress. https://cdn.americanprogress.org/wp-content/uploads/2012/09/StealthInequities_execsumm.pdf

Baker, R., Dee, T., Evans, B., & John, J. (2018). *Bias in online classes: Evidence from a field experiment* (CEPA Working Paper No.18-03). Stanford Center for Education Policy Analysis. http://cepa.stanford.edu/wp18-03

Bass, G., & Lawrence-Riddell, M. (2020, January 20). *Culturally responsive teaching and UDL.* Faculty Focus. https://www.facultyfocus.com/articles/equality-inclusion-and-diversity/culturally-responsive-teaching-and-udl/

Bell, M. (2016, Summer). Teaching at the intersections: Honor and teach about your students' multiple identities. *Learning for Justice Magazine,* 53. https://www.learningforjustice.org/magazine/summer-2016/teaching-at-the-intersections

Borden, A. (2007). The impact of service-learning on ethnocentrism in an intercultural communication course. *Journal of Experiential Education, 30*(2), 171–183.

Borrero, N., & Yeh, C. (2016). Using ecological asset mapping to investigate pre-service teachers' cultural assets. *International Journal of Multicultural Education, 18*(3), 114.

Bourdieu, P. (1986). The forms of capital. In J. Richardson (Ed.), *Handbook of theory and research for the sociology of education* (pp. 241–258). Greenwood.

Buck Institute for Education PBL Works. (2021). *What is PBL?* https://www.pblworks.org/what-is-pbl

Budhai, S. S. (2013). Two sides to every story: Exploring community partners' perspective of their service-learning experiences. *Journal for Civic Commitment, 20,* 1–13.

Budhai, S., & Taddei, L. (2015). *Teaching the 4cs with technology: How do I use 21st century tools to teach 21st century skills?* ASCD Arias.

Carnoy, M., & García, E. (2017). *Five key trends in US student performance.* Economic Policy Institute. Retrieved August 15, 2021, from https://epi.org/113217

Chang, S. (2018, August 30). *Assessing learning in maker education.* Edutopia. https://www.edutopia.org/article/assessing-learning-maker-education

Cheung, F., Ganote, C. M., & Souza, T. J. (2016). *Microaggressions and microresistance: Supporting and empowering students* (Faculty focus special report: Diversity and inclusion in the college classroom). Magna Publication. http://www.facultyfocus.com/free-reports/diversity-and-inclusion-in-the-college-classroom/

Cheung, F., Ganote, C., & Souza, T. (2021, April 7). *Microresistance as a way to respond to microaggressions on zoom and in real life*. Faculty Focus. https://www.facultyfocus.com/articles/academic-leadership/microresistance-as-a-way-to-respond-to-microaggressions-on-zoom-and-in-real-life/

Choi, Y. W. (2020, March 31). *How to address racial bias in standardized testing*. Next Generation Learning Challenges. https://www.nextgenlearning.org/articles/racial-bias-standardized-testing

Christianakis, M. (2011). Parents as "help labor": Inner-city teachers' narratives of parent involvement. *Teacher Education Quarterly, 38*(4), 157–178.

Clark, D. A., Spanierman, L. B., Reed, T. D., Soble, J. R., & Cabana, S. (2011). Documenting weblog expressions of racial microaggressions that target American Indians. *Journal of Diversity in Higher Education, 4*(1), 39–50. https://doi.org/10.1037/a0021762

Clark, P., & Zygmunt, E. (2014). A close encounter with personal bias: Pedagogical implications for teacher education. *Journal of Negro Education, 83*(2), 147–161.

The Condition of Education. (2021). Public High School Graduation Rates. Institutes for Education Statistics and National Center for Education Statistics. Retrieved August 15, 2021, from https://nces.ed.gov/programs/coe/indicator/coi

Crenshaw, K. (1989). Demarginalizing the intersection of race and sex: A Black feminist critique of antidiscrimination doctrine, feminist theory and antiracist politics. *University of Chicago Legal Forum, 1*(8), 139–167.

de Brey, C., Musu, L., McFarland, J., Wilkinson-Flicker, S., Diliberti, M., Zhang, A., Branstetter, C., & Wang, X. (2019). *Status and trends in the education of racial and ethnic groups 2018* (NCES 2019-038). U.S. Department of Education; National Center for Education Statistics. Retrieved August 15, 2021, from https://nces.ed.gov/pubs2019/2019038.pdf

De La Garza, T. O., Lavigne, A. L., & Si, S. (2020). Culturally responsive teaching through the lens of dual language education: Intersections and opportunities. *Universal Journal of Educational Research, 8*(4), 1557–1571. https://doi.org/10.13189/ujer.2020.080450

Derman-Sparks, L., & ABC Task Force. (1989). *Anti-bias curriculum: Tools for empowering young children*. NAEYC.

Duckor, B. (2017). *Mastering formative assessment moves*. ASCD.

Epstein, J. L. (2010). School/family/community partnerships: Caring for the children we share. *Phi Delta Kappan, 92*(3), 81–96. https://doi.org/10.1177/003172171009200326

Eschmann, R. (2021). Digital resistance: How online communication facilitates responses to racial microaggressions. *Sociology of Race and Ethnicity, 7*(2), 264–277.

Fiarman, S. E., & Benson, T. A. (2020). The reality of unconscious racial bias. *School Administrator, 77*(2), 21–25.

Finnerty, D. (2018). Understanding unconscious bias as one more tool in the committed White teacher's equity toolkit. In E. Moore, A. Michael, & M. W. Penick-Parks (Eds.), *The guide for white women who teach black boys* (pp. 55–60). Corwin.

Fleming, L. (2015). *Worlds of making: Best practices for establishing a makerspace for your school*. Corwin.

Franklin, V. P. (2007). The tests are written for the dogs: The Journal of Negro Education, African American children, and the intelligence testing movement in historical perspective. *Journal of Negro Education, 76*(3), 216–229.

Galloway, R., Reynolds, B., & Williamson, J. (2020). Strengths-based teaching and learning approaches for children: Perceptions and practices. *Journal of Pedagogical Research, 4*(1), 31–45. https://doi.org/10.33902/JPR.2020058178

Gardner, H. (2006). *Multiple intelligences: New horizons in theory and practice*. Basic Books.

Gay, G. (2018). *Culturally responsive teaching: Theory, research and practice* (2nd ed.). Teachers College Press.

Gay, G. (2010). *Culturally responsive teaching: Theory, research, and practice* (Multicultural Education Series; 2nd ed.). Teacher's College Press.

Gibson, V. (2020, February 26). *Working towards culturally responsive assessment practices*. National Council of Teachers of English. https://ncte.org/blog/2020/02/working-toward-culturally-responsive-assessment-practices/

Gilliam, W. S., Maupin, A. N., Reyes, C. R., Accavitti, M., & Shic, F. (2016). *Do early educators' implicit bias regarding sex and race relate to behavior expectations and recommendations of preschool expulsions and suspensions?* Yale Child Study Center.

Glossary of Education Reform. (2015, November 10). *Assessment.* https://www.edglossary.org/assessment/

Gonzalez, M., & Kokozos, M. (2019). Prejudice reduction in public schools: A dialogic approach. *Journal of Educational Research and Practice, 9*(1), 340–348.

Gonzalez, N., Moll, L. C., & Amanti, C. (2005). *Funds of knowledge: Theorizing practices in households, communities and classrooms.* Erlbaum. https://doi.org/10.4324/9781410613462

Henderson, A. T., & Mapp, K. L. (2002). *A new wave of evidence: The impact of school, family, and community connections on student achievement.* National Center for Family & Community Connections with Schools. https://sedl.org/connections/resources/evidence.pdf

Henderson, A. T., Mapp, K. L., Johnson, V. R., & Davies, D. (2007). *Beyond the bake sale: The essential guide to family-school partnerships.* New Press.

Hussar, B., Zhang, J., Hein, S., Wang, K., Roberts, A., Cui, J., Smith, M., Bullock Mann, F., Barmer, A., and Dilig, R. (2020). The Condition of Education 2020 (NCES 2020-144). U.S. Department of Education. Washington, DC: National Center for Education Statistics. Retrieved July 2021 from https://nces.ed.gov/pubsearch/pubsinfo.asp?pubid=2020144.

Jacoby, B. (1999). Partnerships for service learning. *New Directions for Student Services, 87,* 18–35.

Johnston, O., Wildy, H., & Shand, J. (2019). A decade of teacher expectations research 2008-2018 : Historical foundations, new developments, and future pathways. *The Australian Journal of Education, 63*(1), 44–73. https://doi.org/10.1177/0004944118824420

Kaul, M. (2019, May 28). Keeping students at the center with culturally relevant performance assessments. *Education Week.* https://www.edweek.org/teaching-learning/opinion-keeping-students-at-the-center-with-culturally-relevant-performance-assessments/2019/05

Kay, M. R. (2018). *Not light, but fire: How to lead meaningful race conversations in the classroom.* Stenhouse.

Kehoe, J. W. (1994). Multicultural education vs anti-racist education: The debate in Canada. *Social Education, 58*(6), 354–358.

Kendi, I. X. (2019). *How to be an antiracist.* Random House.

Kohli, R., & Solórzano, D. G. (2012). Teachers, please learn our names! Racial microaggressions and the K-12 classroom. *Race Ethnicity and Education, 15*(4), 441–462. https://doi.org/10.1080/13613324.2012.674026

Kosciw, J. G., Greytak, E. A., Giga, N. M., Villenas, C. & Danischewski, D. J. (2016). The 2015 National School Climate Survey: The experiences of lesbian, gay, bisexual, transgender, and queer youth in our nation's schools. New York: GLSEN.

Kye, H. (2020). Who is welcome here? A culturally responsive content analysis of makerspace websites. *Journal of Pre-College Engineering Education Research (J-PEER), 10*(2), 1–16.

Ladson-Billings, G. (2014). Culturally relevant pedagogy 2.0: a.k.a. the remix. *Harvard Educational Review, 84*(1), 74–84.

Ladson-Billings, G. (2006). "Yes, but how do we do it?" Practicing culturally relevant pedagogy. In J. G. Landsman & C. W. Lewis (Eds.), *White teachers/diverse classrooms: Creating inclusive schools, building on students' diversity, and providing true educational equity* (pp. 33–46). Stylus.

Ladson-Billings, G. (1994). *The dreamkeepers: Successful teachers of African American children.* Jossey-Bass.

Laher, S., & Cockcroft, K. (2017). Moving from culturally biased to culturally responsive assessment practices in low-resource, multicultural settings. *Professional Psychology: Research and Practice, 48*(2), 115–121.

Lavy, V., & Sand, E. (2018). On the origins of gender gaps in human capital: Short- and long-term consequences of teachers' biases. *Journal of Public Economics, 167*(2), 263–279, https://doi.org/10.1016/j.jpubeco.2018.09.007

Lazar, A. M. (2018). Creating teachers of promise: Growth toward equity-mindedness in a landscape of practice. *Teaching and Teacher Education, 71,* 308–318. https://doi.org/10.1016/j.tate.2018.01.005

Learning Forum SuperCamp. (2016). OTFD: A powerful communication technique. Retrieved April 21, 2021, from https://prezi.com/tszt1slnknpa/otfd-a-powerful-communication-technique/

López, F. (2017). Altering the trajectory of the self-fulfilling prophecy: Asset-based pedagogy and classroom dynamics. *Journal of Teacher Education, 68*(2), 193–212. https://doi.org/10.1177/0022487116685751

Lynch, M. (2016, October 31). How to create culturally responsive assessments. *Education Week.* https://www.edweek.org/education/opinion-how-to-create-culturally-responsive-assessments/2016/10

Manzo, R. D., Rangel, M. I., Flores, Y. G., & de la Torre, A. (2018). A community cultural wealth model to train promotoras as data collectors. *Health Promotion Practice, 19*(3), 341–348. https://doi.org/10.1177/1524839917703980

Mathewson, T. G. (2020). New data: Even within the same district some wealthy schools get millions more than poor ones. *The Hechinger Report.* https://hechingerreport.org/new-data-even-within-the-same-district-some-wealthy-schools-get-millions-more-than-poor-ones/

Menzies, L., Parameshwaran, M., Trethewey, A., Shaw, B., Baars, S., & Chiong, C. (2015). *Why teach?* Pearson & LKCO. https://doi.org/10.13140/RG.2.2.12227.86567

Merriam-Webster Dictionary. (2021). *Mindset.* https://www.merriam-webster.com/dictionary/mindset?utm_campaign=sd&utm_medium=serp&utm_source=jsonld

Moll, L. C. (2019). Elaborating funds of knowledge: Community-oriented practices in international contexts. *Literacy Research, 68*(1), 130–138. https://doi.org/10.1177/2381336919870805

Molnar, A. (Ed.), Miron, G., Barbour, M. K., Huerta, L., Shafer, S. R., Rice, J. K., Glover, A., Browning, N., Hagle, S., & Boninger, F. (2021). *Virtual schools in the U.S. 2021.* National Education Policy Center. Retrieved August 15, 2021, from http://nepc.colorado.edu/publication/virtual-schools-annual-2021

Moloi, T. (2015). Using indigenous games to teach problem-solving in mathematics in rural learning ecologies. *Journal of Higher Education in Africa, 13*(1–2), 21–32.

Morris, M. W. (2016). *Pushout: The criminalization of Black girls in schools.* The New Press.

National Center for Cultural Competence at Georgetown University. (2021). *Two types of bias.* https://nccc.georgetown.edu/bias/module-3/1.php

Ni, Y., & Rorrer, A. K. (2018). *Why do teachers choose teaching and remain teaching: Initial results from the educator career and pathway survey for teachers.* Utah Education Policy Center.

Nieto, S., & Bode, P. (2020). School reform and student learning: A multicultural perspective. In J. A Banks & C. A. McGee Banks (Eds.), *Multicultural education: Issues and perspectives* (9th ed.; pp. 258–276). Wiley & Sons.

Nieto, S., & Bode, P. (2018). *Affirming diversity: The sociopolitical context of multicultural education* (7th ed.). Pearson.

Noddings, N. (2003). *Caring: A feminine approach to ethics and moral education* (2nd ed.). University of California Press.

Okonofua, J. A., Paunesku, D., & Walton, G. M. (2016). Brief intervention to encourage empathic discipline cuts suspension rates in half among adolescents. *Proceedings of the National Academy of Sciences of the United States of America, 113*(19), 5221–5226. https://doi.org/10.1073/pnas.1523698113

Ong, A. D., & Burrow, A. L. (2017). Microaggressions and daily experience: Depicting life as it is lived. *Perspectives on Psychological Science, 12*(1), 173–175.

Ortega, A., Andruuczyk, M., & Marquart, M. (2018). Addressing microaggressions and acts of oppression within online classrooms by utilizing principles of transformative learning and liberatory education. *Journal of Ethic & Cultural Diversity in Social Work, 27*(1), 28–40.

Overton, T. (2012). *Assessing learners with special needs: An applied approach.* Pearson.

Paino, M., & Renzulli, L. (2012). Digital dimension of cultural capital: The (in)visible advantages for students who exhibit computer skills. *Sociology of Education, 86*(2), 124–138. https://doi.org/10.1177/0038040712456556

Papageorge, N., Gershenson, S., & Kang, K. (2020). Teacher expectations matter. *The Review of Economics and Statistics, 102*(2), 234–251. https://doi.org/10.1162/rest_a_00838

Paris, D. (2012). Culturally sustaining pedagogy: A needed change in stance, terminology, and practice. *Educational Researcher, 41*(3), 93–97. https://doi.org/10.3102/0013189X12441244

Paris, D., & Alim, H. S. (2014). What are we seeking to sustain through culturally sustaining pedagogy? A loving critique forward. *Harvard Educational Review, 84*(1), 85–100. https://doi.org/10.17763/haer.84.1.982l873k2ht16m77

PBS. (2020). *Decolonizing our classroom starts with us.* https://www.pbs.org/education/blog/decolonizing-our-classrooms-starts-with-us

Project Implicit. (2011). About the IAT. https://implicit.harvard.edu/implicit/iatdetails.html

Quinn, D. M. (2020). Experimental evidence on teachers' racial bias in student evaluation: The role of grading scales. *Educational Evaluation and Policy Analysis, 42*(3), 375–392.

Rolón-Dow, R. (2005). Critical care: A color(full) analysis of care narratives in the schooling experiences of Puerto Rican Girls. *American Educational Research Journal, 42*(1), 77–111. https://doi.org/10.3102/00028312042001077

Rowe, M. (2008). Micro-affirmations and micro-inequities. *Journal of the International Ombudsman Association, 1*(1), 45–48.

Schwartz, S. (2019). The power of facing our unconscious bias: Diversity training asks teachers to understand students' different backgrounds. Implicit-bias training goes further, and asks teachers to look at themselves. *Education Week, 38*(33), 10.

Scruggs, A. (Fall 2009). Colorblindness: The new racism? *Teaching Tolerance.* https://www.learningforjustice.org/magazine/fall-2009/colorblindness-the-new-racism

Sensoy, Ö., & DiAngelo, R. (2014). Respect differences? Challenging the comming guidelines in social justice education. *Democracy & Education, 22*(2), 1–10.

Shah, N., Ortiz, N. A., Christensen, J., Stroupe, D., & Reinholz, D. L. (2021). Who Participates? Making Equity Work in Classrooms Actionable. *ASCD.* https://www.ascd.org/el/articles/who-participates

Singleton, G. (2014). *Courageous conversations about race: A field guide for achieving equity in schools* (2nd ed.). Corwin.

Slee, J. (2010). A systemic approach to culturally responsive assessment practices and evaluation: Culturally responsive assessment. *Higher Education Quarterly, 64*(3), 246–260.

Sparks, S. (2019). Why teacher-student relationships matter. *Education Week.* https://www.edweek.org/teaching-learning/why-teacher-student-relationships-matter/2019/03

Spencer, S., Logel, C., & Davies, P. (2016). Stereotype threat. *Annual Review of Psychology, 67*(1), 415–437. https://doi.org/10.1146/annurev-psych-073115-103235

Staats, C. (2015). Understanding implicit bias: What educators should know. *American Educator.* https://www.aft.org/ae/winter2015-2016/staats

Starck, J. G., Riddle, T., Sinclair, S., & Warikoo, N. (2020). Teachers are people too: Examining the racial bias of teachers compared to other American adults. *Educational Researcher, 49*(4), 273–284. https://doi.org/10.3102/0013189X20912758

Steele, C. (1999). Expert report of Claude M. Steele. *Michigan Journal of Race and Law, 5,* 439–450. https://core.ac.uk/download/pdf/232704645.pdf

Sue, D. W. (2010). *Microaggressions in everyday life: Race, gender, and sexual orientation.* John Wiley & Sons.

Sue, D. W., Alsaidi, S., Awad, N. M, Glaeser, E., Calle, Z. C., & Mendez, N. (2019). Disarming racial microaggressions: Microintervention strategies for targets, white allies, and bystanders. *American Psychologist, 74*(1), 128–142.

Sue, D. W., Capodilupo, C. M., Torino, G. C., Bucceri, J. M., Holder, A. M. B., Nadal, K. L., & Equilin, M. (2007, May–June). Racial microaggressions in everyday life. *American Psychologist, 62*(4), 271–286. doi:10.1037/0003-066X.62.4.271

Suttie, J. (2016, October 28). Four ways teachers can reduce implicit bias. *Greater Good Magazine.* https://greatergood.berkeley.edu/article/item/four_ways_teachers_can_reduce_implicit_bias

Tatum, B. D. (2003). *Why are all the black kids sitting together in the cafeteria? and other conversations about race.* Basic Books.

Tomasetto, C., Alparone, F. R., & Cadinu, M. (2011). Girls' math performance under stereotype threat: The moderating role of mothers gender stereotypes. *Developmental Psychology, 47,* 943–949.

Tomlinson, C. (1995). How to differentiate instruction in mixed-ability classrooms. Association for Supervision and Curriculum Development.

Torres, F. (2018, January 5). *Managing microaggressions for more inclusive online learning.* https://onlinenetworkofeducators.org/2018/01/05/managing-microaggressions-inclusive-online-learning/

University of Southern California, Center for Urban Education. (2021). *An introduction to the equity scorecard.* https://cue.usc.edu/files/2016/01/Introduction-to-the-EqS.pdf

University of California, San Francisco, Office of Diversity and Outreach. (2019). *Unconscious bias*. https://diversity.ucsf.edu/resources/unconscious-bias

Vygotsky, L. (1978). *Mind in society: Development of higher psychological processes*. Harvard University Press.

Wachira, P., & Mburu, J. (2019). Culturally responsive mathematics teaching and constructivism: Preparing teachers for diverse classrooms. *Multicultural Learning and Teaching, 14*(1), 1–8. https://doi.org/10.1515/mlt-2016-0023

Wang, S., Rubie-Davies, C., & Meissel, K. (2018). A systematic review of the teacher expectation literature over the past 30 years. *Educational Research and Evaluation, 24*(3–5), 124–179. https://doi.org/10.1080/13803611.2018.1548798

Warner, N., Njathi-Ori, C., & O'Brien, E. (2019). The GRIT (gather, restate, inquire, talk it out) framework for addressing microaggressions. *JAMA Surgery, 155*(2), 178–179. https://doi.org/10.1001/jamasurg.2019.4427

Whitford, D. K., & Emerson, A. M. (2019). Empathy intervention to reduce implicit bias in pre-service teachers. *Psychological Reports, 122*(2), 670–688. https://doi.org/10.1177/0033294118767435

Williment, K., & Jones-Grant, T. (2012). Asset mapping at Halifax public libraries: A tool for beginning to discover the library's role with the immigrant community in Halifax. *Partnership: The Canadian Journal of Library and Information Practice and Research, 7*(1), 1–12.

Wren, D. G. (2019). *Assessing deeper learning: Developing, implementing, and scoring performance tasks*. Rowman & Littlefield.

Wright, Z. (2019, October 3). We can't just teach about heroes and holidays and call it culturally responsive. *Education Post*. https://education-post.org/we-cant-just-teach-about-heroes-and-holidays-and-call-it-culturally-responsive/

Yosso, T. J. (2005). Whose culture has capital? A critical race theory discussion of community cultural wealth. *Race Ethnicity and Education, 8*(1), 69–91.

Index

CORWIN
A SAGE Publishing Company

Helping educators make the greatest impact

CORWIN HAS ONE MISSION: to enhance education through intentional professional learning.

We build long-term relationships with our authors, educators, clients, and associations who partner with us to develop and continuously improve the best evidence-based practices that establish and support lifelong learning.

Confident Teachers, Inspired Learners

**CARLA MARSCHALL,
ELIZABETH O. CRAWFORD**
Nurture "Worldwise Learners": students who both deeply understand and purposefully act when learning about global challenges.

**JULIE STERN, KRISTA FERRARO,
KAYLA DUNCAN, TREVOR ALEO**
Harness the critical concepts of traditional disciplines while building students' capacity to transfer their learning to solve novel and complex modern problems.

CHASE NORDENGREN
Demonstrate goal setting as an integral instructional strategy to help students take ownership of their learning.

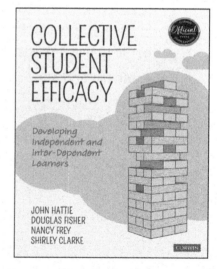

**JOHN HATTIE, DOUGLAS FISHER,
NANCY FREY, SHIRLEY CLARKE**
Working with other people can be a powerful accelerator of student learning and a precursor to future success.

To order your copies, visit **corwin.com/teachingessentials**

No matter where you are in your professional journey, Corwin aims to ease the many demands teachers face on a daily basis with accessible strategies that benefit ALL learners.

CAROL PELLETIER RADFORD

Equip teachers with the tools they need to take care of themselves so they can serve their students, step into leadership, and contribute to the education profession.

STEPAN MEKHITARIAN

Combine the best of distance learning and classroom instruction with a new vision for learning and professional development that capitalizes on the distance learning experience.

SERENA PARISER, VICTORIA S. LENTFER

Find actionable answers to your most pressing questions on how to create and sustain dynamic classroom.

STEPHANIE SMITH BUDHAI, KRISTINE S. LEWIS GRANT

Help teachers pivot instruction to ensure equitable, inclusive learning experiences in online and in-person settings.